THE
ORGANIZATION
GUERRILLA

ALLEN WEISS

THE ORGANIZATION GUERRILLA

PLAYING THE GAME TO WIN

ATHENEUM   NEW YORK

1975

TO *Enid, Sue, Bob*—
AND *Florence,* WHOSE LIFE WAS TOO SHORT

PREFACE

WHILE TESTIFYING before a Senate investigating committee, one bright but distraught young witness was asked what advice he would give to other young people who might entertain thoughts of entering government service. Gordon Strachan answered, almost tearfully, that he would have to advise them to stay away. Contrary advice was offered later by some of the very people who had caused Mr. Strachan's discomfiture in the process of bringing about their own.

This incident runs parallel to the experience of the business world in attempting to attract bright young people from university campuses. Business is at the center of our society, a society dedicated to the pursuit of material progress, technological improvement, and an ever-increasing gross national product. Nevertheless, young people continue to pass the word: Stay away from business and its blandishments.

Indeed, we have heard so much of alienation, dropping out of society, and opposition to the Establishment and to the Organization Man that we are in danger of becoming inured to a situation that ought to call forth our best efforts toward change and improvement. Until significant changes are wrought, however, this book seeks to make a contribution of a different nature. My intention is to help the young, and well-motivated people of all ages, find their way in the system as it stands.

The problems of our society are not confined to business and government. The difficulties individuals encounter have a broader scope. We have, in fact, institutionalized our entire society to the point where the organization has taken over. As a consequence, everywhere we turn we find ourselves contending with organizations and their fundamental law: *Whenever people join together in any activity, some will seek to take advantage of others and of the group's power.* This, then, is the First Law of Organizations. Little wonder that it poses problems for well-meaning people to cope with.

This book does not propose that the individual attempt to tear down the structure, for it would only be rebuilt to meet a set of continuing needs, nor that he turn tail and run, for there is no escape. Government and business affect our lives for good or ill. Whether we like it or not, organizations of all kinds surround us; and we have no choice but to live in the environment they create. Accordingly, the solution proposed here is to arm yourself for the tournament, understand the rules and the risks, and enter into the lists with your banners flying high.

This book will neither sermonize nor moralize. It will prepare young people to enter the (jousting) field of their choice with their eyes open; to see what goes on around them sooner and with greater clarity; to make fewer mistakes; and to reduce their vulnerability and exposure to risk.

At the same time, this book is intended to help those who have started on their way up the ladder, so that they may climb the next rungs with surer footing and greater confidence. Futhermore, since people at all levels do observe and analyze—with or without books like this one—the guidelines set forth here can help those at the upper echelons of the hierarchy to know what sort of perception others are acquiring, and perhaps to fill in gaps they may have missed in their own experience.

Even those whose primary interest lies in volunteer work for charitable or community organizations will find that the rules of the organization apply. Once these people have becomed trained observers, they will discover in their encounters with organizations a fascinating subject for objective study.

Although this book is written primarily for laymen, it contains much material for consultants and students of management to ponder. Experience and observation, abetted by reason, led this study to an irreverent look at management theory. While the Natural Laws and their consequences will be recognizable to people in organizations, the theoretically oriented reader may be startled at the inadequacy of many previously accepted postulates. In the words of Robert Burns, reflection on the Natural Laws of Organizations "wad frae monie a blunder free us/And foolish notion . . ."

Above all, it is the intention of this book to add zest to the game and, we may hope, to play a part in raising strategies and tactics to higher levels of sophistication, as comprehension of the rules spreads out in ever-widening circles. When those who join organizations come equipped with a deeper understanding of the rules, the game will improve. And as the game improves, it will become more interesting to the serious players.

CONTENTS

III INSIDE THE ORGANIZATION

IV POLITICKING FOR SURVIVAL

V COMMUNICATION AND INTERACTION

I

ORGANIZATIONAL BEHAVIOR

1

THE NATURAL LAWS OF ORGANIZATIONS

IT HAS OFTEN been observed that a group at work or play will enforce a code of conduct on its members. Even those volunteers who seek only companionship must relinquish a measure of freedom: They must observe the dos and don'ts of the group.

In more complex structures, narrow objectives are subsumed under broad ones, and the good of the whole is paramount. In the interests of conformity, individual goals are adapted to company objectives. So goes the theory; in practice, it becomes management's responsibility to enforce such *goal-congruence*. The company's will becomes management's guide.

More accurately: *Management's will becomes the company's guide.* In this stressful situation, a struggle is bound to ensue. People on all sides will try to work out angles for themselves. This is not to say that people are lazy, nor that they try to avoid work. On the contrary, they often create both work and hardship for themselves from motives that are selfish and competitive, if not greedy and ruthless.

Out of this conception, the First Law of Organizations is born:

1. THE LAW OF AGGRANDIZEMENT. *Whenever people join together in any activity, some will seek to take advantage of others and of the group's power.*

This fundamental Law underlies most of the other Laws of Organizations. Not only do individuals perversely question managerial decisions (and long to substitute their own judgment), but executives share with—in descending order—managers, supervisors, and the rank and file, an ambivalence toward the company itself. At all levels, people find themselves torn by opposing influences. The urgings of the First Law lead frail human beings to pursue personal aggrandizement, and yet they also feel a responsibility to act in the company's best interests.

However, the Law of Aggrandizement is tempered—in thriving organizations—by another Law based on that responsibility and rooted in self-interest combined with interdependence. The employees of a company have a stake in its survival; and no matter how intense rivalries may become, people who refuse to put their company's (or their group's, or their party's) survival ahead of their own factional concerns risk being shunted aside. This conclusion leads to the rigid Second Law of Organizations:

2. THE LAW OF GROUP SURVIVAL. *The continued existence of the organization must never be imperiled from within.*

Nothing is better calculated to arouse a solid front of active opposition, accompanied by hostility, than a serious threat to group survival. Indeed, the company must not even appear to be threatened with instability; for the mere hint of jobs jeopardized or activities dissolved is intolerable on every hand.

In its simplest terms, this law puts internal disputes on the level of party primaries or conventions. After the issues are settled and the party's candidates are chosen, it is incumbent on the disputants to reconcile their differences and go into the general election with a united party. The alternative raises a threat of defeat, as has so often occurred when a recalcitrant wing of either party sat out an election. In the business world, persistent internal conflict tends to impair a company's competitive position as surely as divisiveness undermines a political party. Thriving companies have invariably recognized this axiomatic truth; and every company had better react swiftly when its survival is jeopardized internally.

To individuals concerned for their own survival, it becomes necessary to avoid incurring the company's wrath. While looking after their own interests, managers and employees alike must always reflect the appearance of company men and women, taking care to put the company first in any plans they present. For instance, Susan Williams wants to expand her own activities in a direction that leads to conflict with someone else. She will, in fact, be stepping on toes. Very well; she must show how the organization will gain from her proposal. There may be a fight. She has to be prepared to stick to her guns: *Her proposal is for the good of the organization.* All other consequences are incidental. And when the battle is over, win or lose, she must take immediate steps to make up with the other side, once more in the interests of the organization. For the sake of harmony, she has to be gracious in victory, a good loser in defeat, going out of her way to cooperate with former opponents.

This strategy of cooperating with opponents can be carried a step further. On noticing a certain coolness or resentment in another person, is it better to let her or him sulk or to patch up the differences? In many cases, the first course is unsound and the second can't be accomplished. But something else can be done. It's a good maneuver to ask an adversary's advice about another matter, like which fishing rod to buy. It may be possible to call him for lunch and talk about his favorite team. Other methods include stopping him in the hall and regaling him with a couple of choice stories, congratulating him on his daughter's graduation, or buying him a drink on the way home. Whatever the tactic chosen, the purpose is to make it difficult for him to nurture enmity —unless he's a thoroughgoing blackguard.

Knowing how to disarm the opposition is a valuable asset, not to be abused by stating opinions strongly or frequently. The company's survival depends on a general willingness to get along together. A reputation as a doctrinaire can hardly help to gain favor, no matter how expert you may have become at smoothing ruffled feathers afterward.

People with Machiavellian leanings will have difficulty evaluating the strategies advanced here, for this book neither recommends nor condones the destruction of opponents out of fear that they will seek revenge. The difference between such methods and the laws that govern modern organizations is akin to the difference between dictatorships and democratic societies. On one hand, authoritarian leadership puts its concern for the leader and his preservation ahead of all other matters, and it ends by destroying real and fancied threats to the leader's continued dominance. On the other hand, democratic leadership depends for survival on the goodwill of the governed, so it proceeds to reconcile differences and placate opponents.

Even as each individual seeks to gain an edge over his associates (the Law of Aggrandizement), he or she must avoid the appearance of endangering the organization by his actions (the Law of Group Survival). In his efforts to gain a disproportionate share of the benefits derived from joint efforts, it would be self-defeating to announce devious intent; so concealment is ordained by the Third Law of Organizations:

3. THE LAW OF RATIONALIZATION. *No one can be counted on to reveal the real reasons for what he does.*

Only the gullible believe the grounds that are offered to justify actions of any sort. Business, government, and even nonprofit institutions are highly market-oriented. They are, in fact, market-oriented in many more ways than are beneficial to the general welfare:

• If advertising people think they can sell more detergent by talking up its color than by explaining its action, then their pitch will concentrate on color, despite its obvious irrelevance.

• If a salesperson believes he can sell himself better than his appliances, he will use the old-buddy appeal to cultivate his customers and load them up with products, some of which, no doubt, are inferior to competing lines (although others may be quite capable of selling on their own merits).

• Once a supervisor has caught on to behavioral theory, she will say things calculated to motivate her staff toward increased productivity, and she won't let facts deter her. To act otherwise would look foolish, if not self-destructive, on her part.

Market-orientation can be defended when it seeks to ascertain the *wants and needs* of actual or potential customers, in order to go about the business of satisfying them better. Thus, if people want portable color television sets, the market-oriented manufacturer makes them available. Indeed, an economy that depends on the market mechanism to function properly, both encourages and benefits from market-orientation in individual enterprises.

An ethical problem arises when *wants* are separated from *needs*, and appeals are aimed at what people fancy. Many people want cigarettes, candy, liquor, tranquilizers—the list is long and opinions differ—but do they need these items? An easy, and quite defensible, solution to the moral issue is to merely accept people, including their presumed wants, as they are. Who is to say, after all, whether another person knows better than Tom, Dick, and Harriet what is best for them? Why should teetotalers impose prohibition on those who find social value in alcoholic beverages? Having accepted other people's prerogatives, it is a short step to cater to their wants, accepted also at face value, and a shorter step to appeal to them on the basis of those wants.

The true specialists in winning people over by understanding their wants, regardless of their needs, are the professional politicians. Watch the competent ones in action. They consistently avoid abstruse reasoning, no matter how valid it may be, in favor of simple—even simplistic—arguments with popular appeal. Many of the top pros have sharp minds; they are fully capable of grasping the significance of recondite theories. But most of all, they grasp the essence of a democratic society: A vote is a vote, no matter who casts it. Furthermore, mediocre voters outnumber the profound thinkers by a wide margin. These observations lead to a corollary, the Fourth Law of Organizations:

4. **THE LAW OF SELF-INTEREST.** *Only egotists favor the reasons they like best, rather than the arguments that convince others and are least vulnerable to counterattack.*

People who are serious about getting a point across, as everyone should be, must plan a strategy from the standpoint of its effectiveness in persuading *other* people. At the same time, one must be cautious of unwelcome consequences to avoid: a backlash that threatens to defeat the effort, or a trap for the unwary. For example, Arthur Gordon came up with an idea for expediting complaints in an office. His proposal would make life easier for the service department, keep the customers happy, and cut costs at the same time. Arthur showed the service department how it would benefit them; he pointed out to the sales department how customers would get better service; and he proved to the budgeteers that expenses would be reduced. Was everybody happy? Not on your life! The service department worried about a cutback; someone's job was at stake. The salespersons suspected a plot to raise their quotas; Arthur did say that their customers would be happier, didn't he? And the budgeteers saw

Arthur as a poacher in their hunting grounds; they were being paid to save the company money, so what did he think he was doing?

What happened? Arthur's arguments were directed at his audience, all right, but not in ways that they could appreciate. He stepped on toes when he should have tread carefully. Arthur could have spared himself trouble by taking a second look at arguments that appeared cogent to him, this time asking how they would sound to his chosen audience. It's always useful to raise such questions as these: Will others understand, or will the rationale sail over their heads? Will others relate to the situation, or will they be indifferent? Moreover, will they see themselves as being threatened?

Perhaps Arthur should have gone higher in the organization. Nevertheless, it is well to consider a characteristic embodied in the Fifth Law of Organizations:

5. THE LAW OF CONSTRAINTS. *No one in any organization has absolute control over any activity or any group.*

Pressures from above and below must be reckoned with. No matter what a person's own intentions or predilections may be, her thinking and her acts come to be dominated by the company. In a sense, she is a prisoner of the Establishment. Additionally, subordinates and peers cannot be brushed aside with impunity. Their expectations demand respect. This law applies even to those who appear to be in full control.

"How can that be?" you may ask. "Surely the president has the power to issue orders and have them carried out." Admittedly things look that way from the outside, where customers and creditors assert prerogatives of their own, but remain unaware of internal pressures. Nevertheless, those orders must be consistent with general expectations. Radical shifts unsettle people and impair confidence in their leaders, even when the groundwork has been laid in advance. Furthermore, even in the most authoritarian organizations (and societies) there is always some jockeying for position. Although rebellion is rare, the possibility of individual defection cannot be lightly dismissed.

More immediately, *the people who keep a company going are not the sycophants who kowtow on cue.* Deep in the consciousness of every executive, there is an awareness that the yes-men would fall apart without him, whereas the strong subordinates would find their own way. Moreover, the strong ones have good advice to offer, and they recognize failure when it occurs. In short, no matter how an executive may try to provide for himself a stable environment peopled by loyal followers, he can never escape the potential threat of a loss of power to more capable hands, if he should falter. Consequently, he feels certain constraints on his power: His own fallibility makes him vulnerable.

The Law of Constraints has its corollary, the Sixth Law of Organizations:

6. THE LAW OF INFLUENCE. *Everyone in an organization has a capability for exerting pressure on others to a greater or lesser extent.*

A boss must concern himself with the views and reactions of his subordinates; therefore, they have a hold on him. They can influence his decisions. An individual with a reasonably good record can influence those around him and those above him in the organization. On occasion, he can get away with jerking the reins of control a little.

The fine art of politicking involves evaluating the relative strength of various positions and negotiating for as much advantage as one's strength commands. Reformers in party politics traditionally shun such tactics, and they pay dearly for their intransigence. Sometimes they succeed in winning all the chips—for a while—but more often they settle for nothing at all when they could have been on the receiving end of a series of modest gains. Unfortunately, too many reformers become quite content to settle into a pattern of losing—honorably, of course, but irresponsibly, too.

While amateur reformers proudly display their badges of purity, professional politicians seek accommodation with those in power. To them, the only loss that is unconscionable lies in settling for less than they should have, given their strength among party workers, contributors, and voters.

The negotiator's approach is generally both more practical and more democratic than the politics of confrontation, with its recourse to displays of raw power, or the underhanded politics of sniping and smearing. Negotiation, compromise, and reconciliation succeed where confrontation and destructive activities generally fail, because the organization's survival is all-important. Stated more broadly, ambitious people in organizations should act toward others with sensitivity, courtesy, and respect. This ennobling thought leads directly to the Seventh Law of Organizations:

7. THE LAW OF FUGLING. *Success in management ranks depends in large measure on fugling with grace.*

All successful managers have one thing in common: They have learned to fugle. A fugleman is the soldier who stands before his company to demonstrate, lead, teach, and guide as his fellows go through such exercises as the manual of arms. The fugling of managers is less immediately obvious but certainly as effective over extended periods. Subordinates make it so. They search for subtle indications of approval or disapproval. They emulate out of genuine respect, copy out of habit, and follow out of loyalty. Even those who resist are generally aware of the manager's role as a fugleperson, and of their own opposition to it.

The typical organization relies on a few hard-working loyalists who know what to do and how to do it, however imperfectly. Most people, at all levels, follow along, content to make modest contributions; while another group flounders, fakes output, and schemes to keep afloat. Here and there, a well-motivated island exists with high morale, little loss of time to nonproductive activities, and no hangers-on. Such a department is frequently respected, more often feared, and always resented. It will be accused of snobbishness and secrecy, partly because its people are probably self-assured and aloof.

Unfortunately, neither departments nor individuals achieve dominant positions in organizations by dint of industrious application of productive energy. They succeed through expert political maneuvers. Politicking, whether it is called handling people, interpersonal relations, gamesmanship, career advancement, opportunism, in-fighting, behavioral theory, or human engineering, is a major—and well-rewarded —activity in all organizations.

The truth is that every executive has, in one way or another, succeeded in playing politics. Each individual has played his own game in a style that reflects his personality. Each has adapted his strategies to suit the circumstances as he perceived them. Accordingly, the successful executive in an authoritarian environment differs from his counterpart in a permissive atmosphere, and the success in retailing differs from her opposite number in manufacturing or government. There is room for a great many individual styles in business.

Something about fugling arouses instinctive envy, often mixed with distrust; and the aspiring executive must be careful to avoid creating resentment unnecessarily. Without projecting an air of diffidence, he must nonetheless acknowledge a debt to others in a special kind of interdependent relation. Since this most important of all managerial arts deserves a name, let us call it *fugling with grace*.

Fugling with grace is a genuine leadership characteristic, essential to anyone who wants to succeed in politicking. Nevertheless, fugling looks downward—and sometimes sideways —in the organizational framework; accordingly, it must be complemented by another view of the power structure: one that looks upward. That view is embodied in the Eighth Law of Organizations:

8. THE LAW OF POWER. *Power follows money: PFM.*

While all the previous Laws are important, and none can be ignored with impunity, this Law of the sources of power has especial significance. The objective—the very essence—of politicking is to acquire power by working through people within the organizational framework. Clearly, one must find the source of power in order to exploit it. Although the statement of the Law—power follows money—is brief and simple, the concept has many facets, which will be explored in the next chapter.

RECAPITULATION

The eight Natural Laws of Organizations provide a starting point for a study of the political strategies that will help individuals survive and prosper in an organizational framework. Specifically, the Laws are useful in analyzing a particular company and evaluating the forces at work within it. Where does power ultimately reside? Which other influences are effective, and which have been ignored? What are the hidden consequences of past actions? How do various individuals operate to gain their personal ends? Who is doing what to whom? What moves can be expected, and when? And always why, why, why: Why did Arthur opt for one course of action instead of another? Why did Susan elect to respond as she did? Why did George choose to say nothing? The Laws are formulated in order to foster an analysis that cuts through the subterfuges directly to the core of each issue.

Additionally, the Natural Laws of Organizations are necessary in plotting your own course, navigating toward personal goals, avoiding the rocks and shoals, and surviving the storms. Difficulties will remain, but surely a knowledge of the rules, the hidden forces, and the motivations of others must accompany any attempt to plan and execute a strategy for survival in a given situation.

In later chapters, we will follow people and events in organizational settings, applying the natural laws implicitly (and sometimes explicitly) to probe in greater depth. For convenient reference, therefore, the eight Natural Laws of Organizations are gathered here:

1. *The Law of Aggrandizement.* Whenever people join together in any activity, some will seek to take advantage of others and of the group's power.

2. *The Law of Group Survival.* The continued existence of the organization must never be imperiled from within.

3. *The Law of Rationalization.* No one can be counted on to reveal the real reasons for what he does.

4. *The Law of Self-Interest.* Only egotists favor the reasons they like best, rather than the arguments that convince others and are least vulnerable to counterattack.

5. *The Law of Constraints.* No one in an organization has absolute control over any activity or any group.

6. *The Law of Influence.* Everyone in an organization has a capability for exerting pressure on others to a greater or lesser extent.

7. *The Law of Fugling.* Success in management ranks depends in large measure on fugling with grace.

8. *The Law of Power.* Power follows money: PFM.

2

WHERE THE POWER LIES

THE INDIVIDUAL who feels herself victimized by system, boss, or organization often asks, "Where can I turn?" Seeking justice, help, or perhaps only a hearing, she finds herself in the predicament of one of Kafka's heroes: unable to get through to someone in authority. Hence the imperative need to know where the power lies. Fortunately, the search for the sources of power need not be conducted in darkness.

The Eighth Law reads, Power follows money: PFM. A simple statement to clarify a baffling riddle. However, the statement PFM itself requires interpretation: It has to be applied to practical situations as they are encountered in the world of organizations. Needless to say, an understanding of the implications of PFM is essential to politicking and survival. An illustration from party politics will cast light on one aspect of PFM.

At a strategy meeting in behalf of a candidate for public office, suburban representatives sat beside a big-city boss. The discussion turned to devices for activating new people in the campaign, and the strategists agreed to organize supporting groups along occupational and professional lines. When the time came to select chairpersons for these groups, the big-city boss proposed or endorsed suburbanites every time. Prestigious appointments were clearly something this party boss could well afford to relinquish.

But when, at other points, paying jobs were under discussion, the same boss showed much greater interest in boosting his city people. The boss's standing in his home grounds depended on his ability to channel funds to the local people.

In politics, keeping an eye on the buck marks the professional, setting him apart from the dilettante; in the company, the play takes on related, but different, shapes. First, the *sources* of money, and the *channels* through which it flows must be uncovered in order to identify the situs of power. Second, an appearance of *conservation* of funds must be maintained in one's own activities, including *cost/effectiveness* (production of benefits in excess of cost) in order to avoid finding oneself declared redundant the next time austerity day rolls around. Third, in the apportionment of company funds, one must garner for oneself sufficient compensation to assure adequate status.

Titles, perquisites, and praise all have their place as indicators of status; but compensation is what establishes that status in the first place. Respect for a person grows with her compensation; the dimensions of her office—and whether she has an office of her own—proclaim approximately what that compensation is. Accordingly, the sophisticated political operative, while not disdaining a large, well-appointed office, will accept no substitute for money. And women must never disengage from battling for equal pay, not only because justice demands it, but also because lower current pay puts one at a disadvantage in the competition for the next upward move. When that longed-for career opportunity opens up, don't risk being denied advancement on the frivolous grounds that it involves "too large a jump for you to make all at once."

THE POWER STRUCTURE

A fact of organizational life is that power follows money: PFM. There are many parallels in everyday living. Proverbs teach that those who pay the piper call the tune, and that the axle must be greased before starting a journey. Economists add that there's no such thing as a free lunch. Since every activity has to be paid for, it follows that each person owes his position to the fact that someone is making funds available to pay for his operation. The providers of funds, whether inside the company or outside, automatically become important persons. Those who work for the company had better make it their business to know who these power-wielders are. By tracing the flow of funds to its sources, you will find, at the headwaters, the principal influences on policy.

In order to set the following discussion on a firm foundation, it becomes necessary to distinguish between two kinds of funds: capital and revenue. Capital funds are intended for investment, whereas revenues come into the company's coffers from the sale of goods and services. Capital funds are typically long-term, whereas revenues are part of the working-capital cycle: Moneys flow in from sales, and they flow out to pay for labor, materials, and operating expenses. The working-capital cycle is relatively short, and it is recurrent. However, our present interest lies primarily in the sources of funds, rather than their uses.

CAPITAL FUNDS

In business, capital funds are of two kinds: equity and borrowed. Corporate equity funds are supplied by stockholders; equity equals ownership. Borrowed funds may come from banks, factors, finance companies, insurance companies, bondholders, and individuals. Distinctions between equity and borrowed funds can be blurred by such devices as *convertible bonds, stock options,* or *warrants* given to a lender as *kickers* to induce favorable action on loans. We needn't be sidetracked by diversions to peripheral issues. Briefly, ownership sometimes matters. For instance, in a dispute between the owner of a company's stock and the bank that lends him money, the stockholder is free to borrow elsewhere—if he can find another willing lender. On the other hand, the bank cannot get rid of the owner, so long as he meets the payments on his loan as they come due.

However, the things that matter most in all circumstances are the amount of money involved, the proportionate share of the whole that a particular stockholder or lender has put up, and the urgency of the company's need for his contribution. Occasionally, a small stockholder in a large company gains notoriety by making loud noises, and he may acquire a nuisance value if his persistent hammering at the Establishment, perhaps in concert with others, leads to reform. In ordinary circumstances, though, the small stockholder's power is virtually nonexistent. *Ownership power is wielded by major stockholders,* who may be officers, directors, investment brokers, fund-managers, or wealthy individuals. These people are not known for giving things away—except as contributions to charity, so designated and tax-deductible.

Underwriters of stock issues frequently demand representation on the board of directors, where they can look after their own interests from the inside. They may hold options or warrants whose value depends on the price movements of the company's stock. (Because of the leverage that inheres in options and warrants, underwriters often bargain for them as part payment for their services.) Other influential stockholders may likewise sit on the board of a public corporation or be represented there by delegates. Furthermore, large lenders can, and frequently do, name directors of their own choosing, especially if a company's troubles in raising money make it weak prey for bullies.

Whether a company is publicly or privately owned, it is not unusual for the financial backers to install their own choice as treasurer, or at least to insist on a voice in selecting financial officers. Whether that state of affairs exists or not, the wise financial executive will certainly want to cultivate the sources of capital funds and their delegates on the board, staying in close touch with them, keeping them informed, and carrying out their wishes. The financial executive who plays this survival game well is not easily discomfited by his colleagues.

Herein lies the answer to a familiar riddle: Why do financial people so often succeed to company presidencies over the heads of marketing people, production people, and others? There has been much speculation concerning the excellent background and training provided by poring over financial data, and also about the unique qualifications of individuals who pursue accounting careers. Nonsense, all nonsense. More figures than anyone could ever need are readily available to executives outside the financial area. Moreover, engineers are credited with logical minds and disciplined thinking; salespersons are considered adept and persuasive in handling people; and leaders in all fields are conceded an ability to get things done. So what is the advantage the financial people have? The inside track; they have access to the providers of capital funds. PFM. Accordingly, nonfinancial persons interested in survival ought to hack out paths of their own to these same sources of power.

REVENUE SOURCES

A consequence of PFM is that the funds a person brings into a company determine her potential for taking money out. Accordingly, it is always useful to be associated with projects and activities that pay their way, and more. For example, in a service organization, it is best to bring in customers, second best to build up "billable time," and poor strategy to do "overhead" work like keeping records. Recognition is enhanced when the payoff is obvious and immediate. Nevertheless, within the potential that is thus established, what anyone actually succeeds in taking away, legitimately, determines her relative status in the pecking order.

Salespersons and others make their way to the top of the corporate pyramid often enough to demonstrate the political importance of revenue sources.

The salespersons who move up in the company are the ones whose sales volumes command respect. However, that observation requires a few words of caution. To be sure, the customers that order the largest quantities are accounted the most important, provided that they also pay their bills promptly. People jump when these customers demand service. Nevertheless, employees of small companies had better heed this warning: An overly large customer becomes a threat to the continued existence of a small supplier, whenever such a customer chooses to press its advantage. Take a few illustrations:

• Mammoth Merchants bought more than half the output of Consumer Products, a small company. The following year, Mammoth compelled Consumer Products to accept a price so low that Consumer barely survived.

• Major Manufacturing found itself unprepared to process an ingredient for a new product in sufficient quantity to meet an extraordinary surge in demand, so it contracted with Local Processors to provide that ingredient in quantity. Each succeeding year, Major's negotiators grew tougher in their price bargaining, until finally Local was compelled to turn Major away. Local managed, in the end, to keep its plant going at adequate production levels and profit margins, but only after a desperate struggle and herculean sales efforts to find replacement customers.

• Tiny Manufacturing became dependent on National Distributors over a long period during which National brought in orders for increasingly large quantities of Tiny's products. When National came along with an offer to buy out Tiny—coupled with a threat to take its orders elsewhere—Tiny threw in the towel. It became a subsidiary of National.

The pattern of these cases is repeated regularly in business. Large customers can make enormous demands, and a customer that is too big for its supplier carries a threat against both the supplier company and its sales representative. Consequently, the salesperson who relies too heavily on one big account is treading on thin ice, and the executive who allows his company to overrate a salesperson on the basis of his success in holding one big account is also asking for trouble.

How then will a salesperson be rated by his company and how will he fare under the rating system? For the most part, salespersons are evaluated and ranked according to the volume they generate, with certain notable exceptions. First, sophisticated managements look to profit margins instead of sales, recognizing that the salesperson who pushes the more profitable products is doing more to enhance operating results than the one who sells merchandise at a discount. Some companies go one step further, evaluating territories on the basis of gross margins earned minus selling expenses incurred. In these companies, a salesperson is well advised to investigate carefully before accepting assignment to a division whose margins are traditionally low. To take an extreme case: Major Processors, with plants in many locations, follows a policy of expanding capacity well beyond current demand. In addition to preparing for anticipated growth, the company's decision-makers believe their policy discourages potential competitors from entering the industry. Perhaps more to the point, the company's labor negotiators argue privately that their bargaining position at contract-renewal time is improved when union representatives for each plant know there is unused capacity at other plants. With a different union at each plant, a strike threat by any one is no threat at all.

Under the circumstances, it is understandable that management should have adopted a permanent policy for building excess capacity. Next, in trying to generate cash flow from excess capacity, the company makes some sales at prices that disregard fixed costs. In a word, Major discounts its products in selling to institutions, while it avoids disturbing regular consumer markets. Any salesperson who undertakes to sell to institutional buyers under these conditions had better know the basis on which he will be evaluated and compensated, for the accountants may report that he is regularly losing money for the company, on a full-cost basis.

Second, some companies set a high value on dependability, and they tend to downgrade salespersons whose volumes fluctuate erratically. This kind of thinking is traceable to excessive planning, which makes a fetish of not having to explain away embarrassing *variances from budget*. When a company is dominated by the budget mentality, salespersons' ratings may be based on *overall performance*, including an evaluation of adherence to plans. So when they find themselves falling below quota, some salespersons call on friendly buyers cultivated through the years for just such emergencies. When one or two of these buyers agree to stock up, ordering in advance of need (in some cases, with shipment to be deferred), sales figures can be brought up to the budget level once again. Needless to say, the salesperson who can swing these deals becomes a favorite of the budgeteers, for there is nothing so dear to their hearts as someone who comes through according to plan. The road to survival for salespersons in such companies is plain enough: Cultivate cooperative customers.

It must not be supposed that the only things that matter are those that are amenable to quantification. Theorists constantly entreat their audiences to eschew such crass thinking. Indeed there are qualitative factors, and these are sometimes influential in determining a salesperson's standing (or anyone else's, for that matter). It doesn't hurt a salesperson to point to prestigious customers in her following. Other things being equal, prominent accounts can earn respect, perhaps envy, among one's associates. Nevertheless, all other things are seldom equal; besides, respect and envy, alas, are not readily convertible into political muscle. PFM: power follows money, not prestige.

ORIENTATION

Despite the validity of PFM, it is too simplistic to conclude that money is everything, and that ownership, selling, or some other source of funds must invariably dominate a company's policies. The fact is that a company's orientation may depend on an interplay among several direct factors, with money determining the outcome only indirectly, often subtly. A few illustrations will clarify this point.

• Techno, Inc., builds better mousetraps. It overwhelms its competitors with engineering skill and production expertise. Needless to say, engineers dominate at the top of the company's structure. They have established personnel policies that contribute notably to the company's success in recruiting and holding high-calibre development engineers. By contrast, the turnover among salespersons is high. But as the engineers say in moments of candor, "Who needs salesmen, when your products are so good?" Salespersons, beware!

• Cut-Rate Company is in a highly competitive industry, and its survival strategy comprises price-cutting to customers and cost-cutting internally. The company's products are sold to industrial customers who show no interest in brand names, relying instead on their own quality control for assurance that specifications are met. Much of Cut-Rate's business comes in response to competitive bids. Production and research executives are all-powerful at Cut-Rate, and the production managers and foremen are protected. By contrast, salespersons and accountants salute when the production people issue commands. More important to ambitious sales and financial people, their career prospects with such a company are dim.

• At Consumer Products, things are different. In this company, market-orientation is complete. Production people often feel browbeaten when a slackening in sales volume leads to charges from the sales force that quality and service have deteriorated, or at least fallen behind in the competition with other products on the market. The badgered production people divert considerable time to defending their operations, but their sporadic counterattacks against sales management cannot change the company's basic orientation. Without such a shift, the climate cannot become hospitable to production managers.

Changes in external situations occur, of course, and they may bring internal repercussions. When raw materials become scarce, purchasing agents find their hands strengthened. In the opposite direction, when overabundance threatens an industry's price structure, a measure of power shifts to those who negotiate collusive agreements to restrict supplies or maintain established price levels (until jail sentences beckon). However, if a situation is perceived as temporary, advantages are not likely to be pushed to extremes, lest severe retribution be meted out later.

In a word, the struggles go on, and an advantageous trend does not automatically augment the fortunes of its natural beneficiaries. They have to overcome their own obedient habits and begin to resist the vested interests of others, risking reprisal at the next spin of the wheel of fortune. Exogenous forces can help a person survive, but only if he seizes his opportunities, keeping an eye out for available new weapons and taking advantage of favorable events.

A company may find itself under pressure from several directions at once. Both personnel and materials may be hard to obtain, in which case recruiters and buyers—one is tempted to say procurers of two types—are both strengthened. Simultaneous attention to processes and cost control is common, and two types of specialist may be forced to acknowledge each other's influence in company affairs: the industrial engineer and the cost accountant. Survival often depends on seeking accommodation with other powerful interests, rather than fighting to the end—probably with the encouragement of bystanders.

The relative strengths of individuals representing diverse interests will depend in part on the force of their personalities. Organizational factors provide opportunities for individuals to exploit, and adeptness in politicking determines the standings of those engaged in the never-ending struggle for power. In a balanced company, each contestant presses his own interests by representing himself as the personification of his department's activities while insisting on a view of the company that moves his department to the foreground. The resultant departmental parochialism creates a certain mystique.

THE DEPARTMENTAL MYSTIQUE

As part of an organizational study, Arthur Gordon interviewed the executives of a company making margarine. Rather than asking bluntly, "What business are you in?" Arthur listened for clues while these people discussed their company's operations, each from his own standpoint. Afterwards, Arthur drafted answers summarizing the positions that developed in the course of many conversations. Here is a sample of those answers:

- The *production* executive's view: "The company refines vegetable oils and converts them into margarine."
- A *buying* executive: "The company buys and sells cottonseed oil and soybean oil. After buying these oils in the commodities markets, we modify them for sale in consumer markets, where we can better dispose of them."
- *Selling*: "The company offers a product that supermarkets and grocers must stock to meet their customers' demands. Among the many brands on the market, we see to it that our brands retain their share of market. We keep retailers well stocked and negotiate for favorable allocations of shelf space."
- *Marketing*: "The company produces popular shows and buys television time for presenting them, thus holding a loyal following of consumers, constituting a market franchise for our products that keeps our plants going."
- *Personnel*: "The company employs people gainfully, contributing to the gross national product and putting money into circulation in the communities where our plants and warehouses are located."

To be sure, executives don't use the precise words Arthur Gordon put into their mouths; but their conversation betrays the rationale he captured. Each executive is predisposed to overrate not only his department, but himself, relative to his associates. Still, it is advisable to demonstrate a correlation between one's own activities and an inflow of company funds. That inflow is a most cogent force in the end.

Accordingly, before joining a company, it is useful to check out its reputation among customers, suppliers, competitors, and the financial community. Find out where the company's strengths and weaknesses lie, for therein lies the key to ascertaining which departments wield the power and which are whistling against the wind. Finally, don't make the mistake of joining a department that's in trouble, unless the proffered job carries full authority to run the department and freedom to act without interference. Even then, the course will be uphill in a handicap race against two sets of competitors: external and internal.

The fight for individual survival begins early, and each decision contributes to victory or defeat. A decision to join a particular department or move to a given location is serious enough to require probing. The departmental mystique is so pervasive that the fact of belonging to one department or another affects one's outlook, thinking, and style.

Each person is expected to exhibit loyalty to her department, adopting a parochial view of the company's activities analogous to the Ptolemaic theory that the universe revolves around the earth. It is not necessary to know whether all of one's associates are true believers in this dedication to local interests, or whether some have reservations. Look at it this way: It gives a person a sense of importance to know that he is part of a department that is carrying the ball for the company. Surely some of the more astute people see through this harmless self-deception, but why deprive anyone of a sense of importance?

The circumstances that give rise to parochialism are not hard to understand. George Roberts may begin as an idealist, eager to pursue noble goals. When he takes a job with Blank Corporation, to earn a living, it is difficult for George to find satisfaction in the thought that his efforts contribute to supplying blanks for conversion by another manufacturer into parts for a machine that makes containers which (before they pollute the environment) carry products that consumers purchase and enjoy. On the other hand, George may be satisfied with belonging to a group which contributes significantly to a company's business—whatever that business happens to be. Thus departments become surrogates on which employees fix their loyalties, in order to acquire, in return, consequence as persons.

There is, to be sure, a perversion of departmental parochialism that troubles practitioners and theorists in management. When the objectives of a department come to be so narrowly defined as to conflict with the overall objectives of the company, executives have something to worry about. This situation is quite common—so common, in fact, that it has been given a name which crops up regularly in management writings: *suboptimization*, the pursuit of local objectives incongruent with corporate objectives. The opposite, a congruence of objectives at all levels, is known as *optimization*.

Since managers are schooled in the dangers of suboptimization, fearful of it, and alert to symptoms of the malaise, it is necessary for individuals to confine departmental enthusiasms to conversations with associates in their own departments. In talking to outsiders, it is advisable to temper that enthusiasm, and to take a broader view of the company's welfare. The sights should be adjusted to each audience in its turn. On moving up the pyramid, the horizon recedes and the view broadens. Petty concerns and departmental loyalties should not be brought upstairs. Listen instead to what is being discussed there, and respond accordingly. Just as with animal species, survival in the company depends on adaptability to *immediate* surroundings.

An excellent illustration of departmental politicking comes from the experts on corporate taxes. To link their function with profit-maximization for the company as a whole, the tax experts begin with the familiar saying "A penny saved is a penny earned." From that start, they continue, "Frankly, we look upon the old saw as an understatement. When the rest of the company earns a dollar of income before taxes, roughly half remains as aftertax earnings; whereas when we save a dollar on tax payments, that dollar belongs to the company in full, for the government cannot claim any of it." Carrying the argument further, the tax experts demonstrate, first, that cost reduction can do no more than increase pretax earnings, which are then subject to the government bite; second, that marketing people may have to produce as much as twenty dollars of revenue to accomplish for the company's earnings what a tax specialist can do with a single dollar's worth of tax-avoidance.

Engineers and research scientists may find solace in reflecting on the social value of their contributions. (Their survival factor would improve if they were to concentrate instead on the dollars of new-product sales their efforts produce.) A salesperson may seek comfort in the thought that he brings in funds to pay the salaries of others, so that they may earn a livelihood. (He's talking money, and that's good for survival.) But tax experts unabashedly cite the bottom-line effect of their work. So cogent is this argument that all other persons must count themselves lucky to find so few tax experts, relative to marketing, operating, and administrative personnel. In the typical corporation, the dulcet sounds emanating from the tax department are drowned out by the more numerous and persistent drum-beaters in other parts. It is nonetheless true that tax specialists offer a superb model for survival.

NONBUSINESS SITUATIONS

An interesting situation—by no means a paradigm—exists in many *professional firms*—partnerships of professionals such as accountants or engineers—that disdainfully refuse to acknowledge the preeminent position occupied by sources of revenue. Professional codes of ethics forbid advertising, promotion, and self-aggrandizement. Practice-development is permissible, and it may include publication of house organs for outside distribution, participation in business and community affairs, or speeches and seminars given by partners. These activities give highly qualified people a chance to build their credentials in impeccably professional ways. Nevertheless, at the moment of truth, a sale is closed by a persuader sitting opposite a decision-maker.

By enjoining themselves from hiring persuaders as sales-persons, professional firms put themselves in an anomalous position. They can hire technically competent practitioners for their staffs; they can retain theorists from the universities; they can bring in specialists as consultants; but they cannot call on the services of salespersons as such. The result of this curious state of affairs is entirely predictable: Among qualified practitioners, a disproportionate allocation of the accolades, along with the lion's share of the earnings, goes to those who sell the firm's services. The mere "technicians" of undisputed competence are not only replaceable, but they are also generally considered to be less valuable to the firm than the PD (practice-development) partners—and the PD types always reach the partner level. Incidentally, administrators also go unrecognized until impending disaster compels grudging, often temporary, reliance on their special skills.

This topsy-turvy condition is the ineluctable outcome of a high-minded refusal to concede that the wheels must be oiled. Even a firm of dedicated professionals must pay its bills and provide its partners with an income. Once again, power follows money: PFM. The lesson is clear: Successful politicking requires that the ambitious professional concentrate more on selling, less on technical competence or knowledge of subject, and not at all on *overhead* activities (like administration) that bring no money into the firm's coffers.

In common with all others, the *nonprofit* organization depends on funding for its continued existence, but its sources are different from those of business. Those institutions that depend on private contributions are dominated by fund-raisers and large donors, whereas those that rely heavily on government agencies turn power over to people who know how to obtain grants, and trade associations would be subject to capture by industry leaders but for the prohibitions imposed by antitrust laws.

Power lines are frequently concealed. It may take a while

to unearth the family relationships between administrators and fat cats. Bide your time; it will all come out. Meanwhile, in dealing with institutions, and especially in working for them, it's best to avoid conflicts with the people at the top. Remember that, by and large, they owe their positions to neither competence nor intelligence nor energy. They hang on within these nonprofit organizations because they have access to the sources of money. Again, PFM.

Government funds come mainly from tax-collections. Nevertheless, power resides not with those who pay taxes, but rather with those who legislate to raise tax money and to spend it. A firm grip on the purse strings is what every politician can understand as a source of strength.

Little wonder then that bureaucrats (the term is not used pejoratively here—these are the people who keep the governmental machinery going) look to legislative bodies and budget administrators for their cues. Of these two groups, the legislators are closer to the people, who elect them, so it may be that democratic processes are served after all when employees of an executive department in local, state, or federal government set about pleasing legislators in order to obtain funding for proposed projects. Provided, of course, that the approaches are honorable and the presentations are reasonably straightforward. In any case, the career government employee, interested in survival, had better not forget that budgeteers shuffle the cards and legislators deal the hands. The good hands go to those who cooperate: PFM.

II

THE
INDIVIDUAL'S
OPTIONS

3

THE JOB SEARCH

ARTHUR GORDON began his career with a professional firm, switching later to a large corporation. A believer in personal contact, Arthur traveled extensively to the company's far-flung locations, partially to evaluate the sincerity of people he dealt with. He had many opportunities to talk things over with people of diverse backgrounds. While observing the politicking of others, he wrestled with his own "people problems," carried the ball for the home office, and reported from the hinterlands after each trip.

At that stage in his career, Arthur hankered for a position "offering greater responsibility and a chance to direct a major operation at close range." In other words, he wanted more money and less travel. He was also unhappy with his autocratic boss. Still, Arthur was in no hurry. It was important to him to make the right move. A few friends knew of his intentions, and they facilitated his job search with recommendations to management consulting firms specializing in executive recruitment.

After a hitch in the Navy, George Roberts went to work

for a small company in his home town. When the company was later acquired by a larger one, George survived the ensuing dismissals and relocations. In a few months, he was promoted. Yet a restlessness developed inside him. He suddenly became acutely aware of his limited experience after contact with headquarters experts. Nevertheless George learned what he could from his new associates and from his trips to the home office. In time, a burgeoning self-confidence emboldened George to seek fresh challenges. In simple terms, he wanted more money and a faster track. Lacking contacts, George answered display ads in major business newspapers, and he registered with a limited number of employment agencies.

Susan Williams had outgrown her small company. Although she held a responsible job, she was impatient to improve her way of life and obtain the recognition she had earned. To put it baldly, she wanted more money, possibly "a piece of the action"; and she was willing to explore possibilities with all comers, large or small. With few misgivings, Susan fearlessly broadcast her availability to friends, acquaintances, business contacts, and associates in a variety of organizations. She was not concerned that her boss might discover her intentions; he already knew them, and he was gambling that Susan would not be able to leave in the end.

Despite differences in their backgrounds, Arthur, George, and Susan shared many experiences in their separate quests. They also felt in common a sense of relief at being unburdened of the troublesome aspects of the jobs they had left behind. Out from under a tyrannical régime, Arthur looked forward to having things done his way. George shook off the uncertainties of dealing with the remote center of power that had manipulated his fate. Susan was relieved of the harassment she had resented.

Setbacks must be expected, of course. Arthur's dream would run afoul of the Law of Constraints: he would never be able to impose his desires on others, willy-nilly. There would always be people for him to persuade and cajole. George would never be entirely free of uncertainty. The Law of Rationalization would keep him from knowing what was going on behind the scenes. Susan would never find rewards coming her way without a contest. The Law of Aggrandizement would stand in her way, until she learned to utilize two other Laws, those of Power and Fugling.

However, the promise and disappointment lay in the future. On making their changes, the three could expect first to feel a strong sense of loss as they found themselves in unfamiliar surroundings, deprived of the greetings, the chats, the banter of former associates. Romanticizing the old, a sense of loss, a fear of the unknown, and a haunting fear of failure produce recurrent doubts in people who change jobs: "Am I doing the right thing? Will I be able to handle my new assignments? Will I be accepted?" Arthur, George, and Susan would ask these questions often.

Meanwhile, there were preliminary steps to be taken. First, the three would be interviewing, and they would make comparisons as to industry, size, location, philosophy, tempo, and financing.

SELF-MANAGEMENT: A FRESH START

A person preparing for an employment interview may find herself faced with this problem: She may perceive that she is dealing with an adversary, she may understand exactly what countermoves she should make, and yet she may find it outside her "nature" to do what has to be done. Still, she must break away from old patterns and adopt new techniques.

This problem of self-management can be difficult. If it happens to be your problem—and it is quite common—you will need to work at a solution. It may help to see yourself as an actor in a make-believe show. Picture yourself stepping into a part in a play. Think of the person who could play that part best, and rehearse an imitation of that person. Frequent rehearsals will familiarize you with the role and remove the awkwardness that accompanies a first trial.

Of course, if the role is one you don't want to be associated with, you shouldn't undertake to play it. But if you can picture yourself in the role with a certain satisfaction, then there is no hypocrisy involved in playing it out: Underneath it all, that role is you. Dare to dream and to act out your dreams. *Your parents, teachers, bosses, associates, and acquaintances had no right to impose on you a personality that never was really yours.* When you explode it, a whole new world could open for you, complete with friends who accept you truly. And you will have attained maturity—which is not synonymous with old age.

EMPLOYMENT INTERVIEWS AND INTERVIEWERS

Although interviews are set up by companies for the purpose of screening out undesirable characters and selecting people who can be counted on to conduct themselves properly, get along with others, and loyally promote the company's interests—objectives that are often incompatible— the job applicant should come to an interview with two purposes of his own: to find out as much about the company as he can, and to tell the interviewers what they want to hear. This application of the Law of Self-Interest is not meant to suggest lying. What is required is to present, as it were, a snapshot of oneself posed at the most favorable camera angle, under the most favorable lighting, in a way that conceals blemishes (which are only superficial, anyhow).

In large companies, where personnel functions are in the hands of specialists, interviewers are committed to implementing management policy, or they wouldn't hold their jobs for long. In other words, a company's interviewers, their boss, and their boss's boss are practiced in putting a good front on everything while concealing everyone's true motives. They live the Law of Self-Interest every day, even when they become disarmingly frank.

It would be more accurate to say that interviewers become especially dangerous when they seek to disarm by an appearance of frankness. A personnelist who is on that kick must never be trusted! The game is to play along, meeting semblance with pretense. The applicant must look open, candid, spontaneous, always taking care that everything he says will help his cause. That's not as easy as it sounds. A skilled interviewer will throw a candidate off guard and then pounce with a quick question. To answer spontaneously without putting oneself in jeopardy can be difficult—but not if the answers are prepared and rehearsed in advance. Now, when an interviewer asks, "What don't you like about your job?" the answer comes promptly: "There isn't enough work to do." If the job to be filled calls for a great deal of contact with the public, an intelligent answer would be that one's present job is too lonely; opportunities to work with other people are infrequent.

To criticize a former employer directly is considered gauche. The stated reasons for leaving must be polite, proper, and sophisticated. Anything less is quite unacceptable. Perhaps a halo on your head is unnecessary, but horns must never appear. Even here, however, opinions differ on some issues. Take for example the charged-up, superaggressive type who insists that he must leave his present job because he needs a faster track, even though he has received a succession of promotions and raises. Some companies will claim to welcome such a fire-breathing world-beater, but most individuals shy away from bringing a dangerous dragon into their midst. Most likely, one executive after another will suggest that this candidate be considered for a different department or, preferably, a division a thousand miles away; and they will give such reasons as his apparent liking for another climate, his supposed background in an esoteric field where experienced people are hard to find, or a mysterious blood chemistry that others are presumed to cherish.

While interviewing, these executives will concentrate on background outside their own fields, to redirect the applicant. "What are you particularly interested in?" means "Where would you rather go than in my department?" When that question comes an applicant's way, his answer should bring the interview right back to the job that he knows is open. And when curves come from the opposite direction, "What don't you do well?" or "What was your weakest subject in school?" safe answers range from oboe-playing to mountain-climbing—except, of course, when applying for a job as a musician at a ski resort.

In fairness to interviewers, it must not be supposed that all their questions have a negative thrust. On the contrary, the best beginners earnestly try to look for positive indications that a candidate will succeed in the job. That's their starting point. Along comes a parade of candidates for various positions—many more people than there are openings—and every candidate presents his credentials in the most favorable light. (Exceptions to this pattern are naïve or self-destructive.) An interviewer who began by looking for positive signs soon learns that she can turn in a superficially acceptable performance by sniffing around for negative indicators instead. This discovery is reinforced when she sends her screened applicants to operating managers for additional interviews. Every time these people uncover derogatory scraps of information, they will deride the poor interviewer, until she finally succumbs to the First Variation on Gresham's Law: *Bad practices drive out the good.* Should the interviewer's conscience and obstinacy prompt her to move to another organization—where the experience is likely to be repeated anyway—the Second Variation on the law will have triumphed: *Inferior people drive out the good.* In either case, *the interview process inexorably turns from selection to elimination.* The successful candidate is seldom chosen in a positive manner, for his potential. He has generally survived a negative process of attrition, by covering his shortcomings.

Companies prod their personnel departments in many ways, creating problems for interviewers to cope with. George Roberts never knew it, but one of those problems knocked him out of a management trainee job he wanted. When George presented himself, the welcome mat was dusted off for this Navy veteran with an unblemished record, good credentials, and superb presence. Articulate and affable, George got along well with his interviewers. But he never got the job, and he was never told the real reason why, for to tell him would have been embarrassing to the company. George was thirty, and the company's top management had decreed, sub rosa, that trainees must be under twenty-six. George was too old. All he heard was that someone else had come along with qualifications that more nearly matched what the company was looking for. The Law of Rationalization at work.

Not all companies would have considered George too old at thirty. For many jobs, he would have been considered too young, despite his qualifications. That sort of thing happens when management becomes concerned about difficulties in hiring competent people, because avenues of promotion are blocked by others younger, or only a few years older, than themselves. The point is that companies continue to discriminate on account of age, among many other factors, and that interviewers are still required by their companies to cover their tracks. Indeed, the more laws there are against discrimination in employment, the more violations there will be, the more covering up, and the more unconscious bias, as personnelists and others struggle to reconcile their own beliefs with the outrageous price their companies put on individual survival. Such a situation can hardly be said to promote honesty, and that's one of the messages the Law of Rationalization is broadcasting. If governments were to pursue rigid law-enforcement policies in all aspects of corporate employment practices and other activities, a bonanza would descend on the criminal lawyers.

The origins of some personnel-department problems are obscure. Somehow it has come to be accepted that, in general, people should expect an increase in salary of no more than 20 percent when changing jobs. There are exceptions of course—notably when a relocation is involved, or when an executive recruiter, affectionately known as a head-hunter, calls. It is bad form to betray eagerness initially; it is not necessary to divulge present income; and it is foolish to sell oneself cheap. Nevertheless, companies seem to agree that, in general, a 20 percent increase should be enough to lure unhappy people away from their employers.

If a person feels himself to be badly underpaid, so that he must have more than a 20 percent increase, interviewers, by common consent, are willing to stretch a point—provided that the applicant does his part. Overstating current income by some 15 to 25 percent is acceptable, and often expected. Most employers wink at this deception by neither issuing nor confirming a salary figure, unless the point is stretched too far. In other words, if one personnelist asks another whether an applicant's salary is in the $20,000 range, and he has actually been paid $18,000, the response will confirm the range. But if an applicant were to claim a salary of $30,000 while actually receiving $18,000, word would be passed that the claim is out of line, even though company policy may forbid divulging salary information to outsiders (a common policy).

Asking too little—a raise of less than 15 percent, for instance—can lead interviewers to suspect someone's motives for leaving. They reason that he may be in trouble. Why else would he take on, for so little reward, the sacrifices, hardships, and risks involved in making a change? Asking too little may be perceived to indicate a lack of self-confidence or self-esteem—very bad in a junior executive or a management candidate. As bad, in fact, as not recognizing your own worth.

When managers find themselves with unanswered questions, they sometimes seek to hire people who have worked for competitors. One candidate may know the terms of an agreement between a competitor and its principal supplier; this information can be used to negotiate better deals. Another candidate may know why a certain buyer regularly favors a particular competitor. Are there personal reasons? With luck, an applicant may turn up who knows how a competitor prices its new products. Such information can be helpful in putting price tags on one's own entries.

An experienced interviewer can often elicit information from novices without having to hire them. A great many business secrets are divulged or corroborated by innocent job-seekers straining to make a favorable impression. In an extreme case, a vice president conducts interviews solely to unearth information. Always fearful of his competitors' plans, he tries to find out what projects are on their drawing boards for products, plants, and territories. He wants to know the names of high scorers on rival teams, and the solutions other companies have devised to problems that are troubling him. All this information is valuable, yet an unwary candidate may give it away free; and those who benefit from such unwitting generosity are not in the least troubled at the thought of wasting people's time, taking them out of their way, and causing them to suffer rejection in the end.

Yet such executives and their companies do hire people, and there may be a reason for wanting an offer from one of them. Be assured that giving away information gets a candidate nowhere. Reticence is a better strategy. An applicant can properly declare certain areas out of bounds, show concern for past employers' interests, and indicate the extent of her knowledge in roundabout ways only.

Invidious interviewing practices conspire with a job-seeker's natural doubts to damage his self-confidence. No one else has quite the same perspective on things that he has. Certainly no one else has nearly the same opportunities for observing his shortcomings. Nor does he have the same opportunities others have to examine and exaggerate *their* weaknesses. In sizing up the people on the other side, it is altogether too easy to overlook their susceptibility to judgmental errors, inadequate planning, and poor execution. To put it less delicately, there are plenty of fatuous, inept people out there, and there are people who are compelled to proceed on the basis of inadequate information. Some of these incompetents are a job-seeker's competitors. Unfortunately, other *incompetents will be interviewing, evaluating, and making decisions.*

These (perhaps) reassuring concepts boil down to the thought that no one has to be perfect to win. Nor is it necessary to have every eventuality covered in advance, whether one is applying for a job or politicking for advancement. On the contrary, to a significant degree, you are justified in relying on the mistakes of others to help you carry the day. Nor is it necessary to go out of your way to capitalize on others' mistakes by setting traps for them. Consider for a moment the strategy of those who survive by staying out of the spotlight, making neither positive nor negative contributions to their companies' welfare, but simply allowing others to fail. The successes of this strategy are attributable to mastery of the art of fugling, assisted by competitors' propensities for committing errors. In ordinary circumstances, it is safe to rely on a combination of the reasonable foresight one possesses and the human frailty of the opposition, without underrating them, and without overdoing one's preparation for every contest.

THE SALESPERSON'S ADVANTAGE

George Roberts's presence and articulateness brought him offers of sales jobs that piqued his interest and led him into discussions with prospective employers. If George chose a career in sales, he would spend considerable time on the road. Excellent food and lodgings would be his due, to assuage the burdens of a traveler's life. On the gloomy side, separations from his family would affect George, his wife, and his children. Of excitement, there would be precious little. The personal advantages of traveling take a different form.

George could expect to meet other salespersons at conventions and on the road, as they covered the same territories and stayed at the same hotels. The inside dope and gossip these people commonly swap about colleagues and competitors is sometimes useful to their companies, and hence to their standings within their companies, but more often it serves personal needs. For instance, they learn of job openings, and when they don't go after one themselves, they often find it advantageous to steer friends in the right direction. Alternatively, letting one's boss in on such a discovery permits him to infer whatever he pleases about the possibility of losing the informant to a competitor. People do get raises that way, as fortune smiles on those who work the angles.

Additionally, members of the informal brother- and sisterhood of salespersons broaden their contacts over the years, a fact that gives them ready access to people who are in a position to help those seeking a change. Indeed, it is often sufficient merely to put out the word that one is unhappy where he is and could become available if the right opportunity presented itself. With no more than a few well-placed telephone calls, a good salesperson can launch a discreet search that widens out on its own. Furthermore, sales contacts work in odd ways, sometimes bringing information about one's own company. For instance, when secret negotiations could jeopardize individual careers, salespersons are likely to get the word first, on the outside. For all these reasons, salespersons are generally better prepared than others to land on their feet when they run into adversity.

Salespersons have other advantages as well. First, aggressive persons with well-developed persuasive talents hold an advantage over more pedestrian types. Second, whether they rely on affability, knowledge, quick thinking, humor, or a good pitch, persons who are confident of their ability to sell themselves convey a self-assured manner that will often carry the day. Third, competent salespersons have learned to "read" people: sizing them up, noting their likes and dislikes, figuring how best to appeal to their vanity as well as their legitimate interests. They know how to listen and observe, and they have developed a sensitivity to the subtle reactions of others. These talents enable them to press advantages, retreat from danger, and alter course—all with correct timing. Fourth, successful salespersons have long ago learned to deliver "little white lies," sometimes called business lies, with an appearance of sincerity.

All these factors—aggressiveness, self-assurance, sensitivity, timing, lying with conviction—work for the salesperson and the sales manager, along with several additional advantages. To begin with, their results are more readily discernible to outsiders and more definitely measurable than the effectiveness of people in production, finance, or data-processing. Rival companies have each other's top salespersons spotted; not so with factory and office personnel. Sales managers make it their business to know which competing salespersons have which accounts in their pockets, who built up what territories, and who swung the big, imaginative deals. By contrast, the production manager who boosted output in his plant cannot expect that other companies will have heard of his feat, nor can the systems analyst who showed her company how to save sizable sums of money.

In short, a variety of factors put salespersons in a most

favorable position to take full advantage of the Law of Influence. A salesperson need not be extraordinary to have an impact on policy in his department and company. Characteristics and situations contrive to give an ordinary salesperson far greater influence than ordinary people in some other activities. When George Roberts, though sorely tempted, chose to resist, he had an excellent reason: Selling was not his passion.

ASSISTANCE FROM OUTSIDE

Susan Williams discovered a way to reach her confrères in business from another base: She joined associations in her field and her industry. A confirmed joiner, Susan could also be found in community organizations, the local political club, and anywhere else that people met. Having noted that much information was swapped at business gatherings, and many contacts could be made there, Susan went a step further, gaining prominence in association work. First she got herself appointed to a committee; then she participated actively in the committee's work, taking assignments cheerfully and carrying them out faithfully. She observed all the standards of behavior for committee members and, when her turn came, chairpersons. Through it all, she cultivated contacts. That wasn't difficult, because committee work involved joint efforts, and also because the people Susan met on committees were thinking along the same lines as she. They understood the game, and they wanted to make contact themselves. In time, one's associates in committee work may become much more than mere sources of information. They frequently show an interest in each other's careers and lend a helping hand at critical junctures.

Every gathering, whatever its basic purpose, serves also to bring together people with similar interests. Accordingly, Susan has found it useful not only to belong to business associations, but also to enroll in courses and seminars, often coming away with valuable acquaintanceships. In a sense, Susan has conducted a perpetual, low-key jobhunt. There's nothing wrong with that, provided one avoids the reputation of being on the make.

Arthur Gordon was fortunate in having been approached by head-hunters conducting searches for executives to fill positions with client companies. Since these recruiters like to work on recommendations, Arthur's meticulous care in personal relations paid off. When the head-hunters called, some at his home and some at his desk, to ask about his interest in making a change, they ordinarily named neither the sources of their information about Arthur nor the companies they were recruiting for. In one case, the source and the company were one and the same. In that instance, a company knew of Arthur and wanted him, but it was reluctant to show its hand, so it consented to the payment of a consulting fee in order to protect itself from a charge of pirating personnel. A consultant overtured Arthur, while the company looked the other way. Such conniving is commonplace in business.

Although Arthur was recommended to head-hunters by his friends, executive recruiters don't work from unsolicited recommendations exclusively. They advertise openings and call people on their list to recommend other qualified people for specific jobs. (Some executive recruiters are mere fronts for employment agencies forbidden by license regulations to approach people not registered with them.) In addition, jobseekers take the initiative, flooding recruiters with résumés. It does no harm to put yourself on file with an executive recruiter, but it's better to have a recommendation.

SWITCHING INDUSTRIES

Early in his career, Arthur Gordon moved easily from a professional firm to industry. A client company offered him a managerial position, and he accepted. His credentials were, of course, in good order. To his outstanding scholastic record, he had added affiliation with a respected firm and the training that that affiliation implied. Arthur's record is even better now, in a sense. He has accumulated knowledge and understanding in many undertakings, and in a particular industry. But therein lurks hidden danger.

From the time Arthur joined his industrial employer, wherever his résumé turned up, he was automatically tabbed as a specialist in his company's industry. Working for a food-processor causes a person to belong to that industry. Joining a food-service company or a retailer stamps one with this designation or that. Being thus labeled, a candidate finds it quite difficult to convince prospective employers that he can carry over sufficient knowledge and skill to perform better than people already in their industry.

Consequently, *it is exceedingly important to choose not only an employer, but also its industry.* Before accepting an offer of employment, it is essential to ask many questions about the industry. How does it rate from the standpoint of enlightened personnel policies, social responsibility (assuming an applicant's concern with social responsibility), and honorable treatment of people? What are its prospects? Is its growth or stability likely to be damaged by technology or legislation that is foreseeable? It isn't enough to know all about a single company; it is essential to know what the industry is like and where it is headed.

Assuredly, the situation is not irretrievably lost with a single mistake—only more difficult. An attempt to change from one industry to another involves stressing those skills and kinds of experience that have obvious carry-over value. Also, the buzz words of the new industry should be learned, and a facility acquired in talking knowledgeably about its problems, patterns, and trends. Waiting for a favorable job market is especially advisable when switching industries. And it is doubly important to avoid compounding mistakes, because mistakes are cumulative, and they reflect on one's judgment when trying for still another change.

One more word of caution. Businessmen's prejudices against government bureaucrats run so high that it is especially hard to move from civil service to industry. To many business interviewers, government workers are a shiftless lot, lacking a concept of a fair day's work. Before accepting a job in government, therefore, it is well to ask oneself what the prospects will be for getting out later. Sometimes, of course, the answer is favorable. Former Internal Revenue Service people are welcome as tax experts, some former military personnel are useful to defense contractors, and persons with experience in certain regulatory agencies often find their way into the industries they regulate. Despite the speculation of suspicious minds, these moves can be entirely legitimate.

4

RUNNING
THE GANTLET

To change jobs is to run the gantlet, with past associates and records lined up on one side and prospective associates on the other. Among the techniques employers past and future resort to in flagellating job-changers are ritual performances like the exit interview, investigation by means fair and foul, and branding of candidates with the characteristics of their employers.

REFERENCES

When Arthur Gordon prepared to change jobs, he took the precaution of verifying that his references were in order. No matter how circumspect one may be in his relations with others, it is unwise to place too much reliance on reciprocal goodwill. Arthur reasoned that he could not know what malicious stories might have been circulated behind his back. Others undoubtedly perceived him as a competitive threat to their careers, and they might have countered that threat by saying things calculated to make him look bad. Moreover, an altogether human boss might have reacted to Arthur's departure as to a personal rejection. Sometimes a cynical executive, finding himself under pressure to defend a high turnover, will resort to defensive tactics that denigrate those who leave. "We're better off without Arthur. He never fit in anyway," translates readily into inadaptability or difficulty in getting along with others.

Direct accusations of incompetence are infrequent, partly because they are questionable in the face of highly favorable periodic evaluation sheets. However, wily executives can surmount this obstacle, too. Some keep private files of all the errors, follies, and doubtful suggestions made by managers and supervisors in their divisions. If necessary, a boss can put these files on display while professing astonishment that the departing person had fooled his superiors for so long. "The truth will out, and so will Arthur; for which I am thankful," can be as damaging as it is unfair.

An additional ploy used by executives calls for shifting a threatening employee frequently. When the discouraged rising star submits a voluntary resignation after a short period in his latest assignment, it can always be said that he was not suited to the demands of his new responsibilities.

What happens when the personnel department dutifully records a malicious final evaluation? Someone may possibly object, in which event the personnelists will huddle to decide whether to pass a timorous query to the evaluator: "Did you mean this?" The critic may then elect either to ignore the issue or to surrender one of his prerogatives. If he opts to do nothing, there will be a permanent stain on the records, and when an inquiry comes from a prospective employer, the answer will reflect the damaging statements in some way.

Sophisticated companies make their inquiries orally, over the telephone, so as to encourage freer expression of damaging statements, which they value highly. Other companies, perhaps because they assess reference checks lightly, send out form letters and get back written responses. In either case, personnelists have plenty to think about when issuing references. To be sure, ethical questions are readily rationalized; few people in business are troubled by them. But legal problems can arise when a defamed person's career suffers injury. The personnelist feels constrained to comply with a directive from his boss to issue references in accordance with the views of authorized executives; the question is how to avoid legal difficulties while the personnelist protects himself from a possible charge of noncompliance with company rules.

Aware that lawsuits can result from damaging references, personnel people resort to a number of subterfuges in their pursuit of the Law of Self-Interest:

• Damning with faint praise is an ancient tactic. Nothing derogatory is said, but a former employee's claim to exceptional qualifications is effectively destroyed by strong hints of mediocrity. "His performance under close supervision was satisfactory, and he could have stayed in his job with the company," is not the way a person might want his reference to read, nor is it the kind of reference he has earned.

• Seemingly innocuous statements with double meanings are a useful ploy. When asked whether a former employee would be rehired, the ex-employer can truthfully answer No, if there is a company policy against hiring former employees. If the recipient of such a reference infers something about the applicant, that mistake can cause the innocent to suffer; but no one can point a finger at the source.

• Helpfulness offers a great escape route. "He is exceptionally competent in certain areas; but the job you describe is not for him." There are variations on this theme. "She wouldn't be happy in your field." "He is at his best when he has complete authority. He feels hemmed in by an organization." The more sympathetic this sort of reference can be made to sound, the more destructive its impact.

In spite of it all, people do change jobs. It is fair to say that, for the most part, references do not stand in the way. Still, it is wise to protect yourself from possible difficulties. Unwilling to accept assurances, Arthur arranged for a friend in a suitable position to check his references. Briefed on the questions to ask and the answers to give, if questioned in turn, the friend called from a business telephone, in case the other party shrewdly wanted to call back, on the pretext that he had people in his office at the moment (standard personnel-department procedure). Arthur's references turned out to be acceptable, but he was prepared to evaluate them objectively, as a stranger might, without straining to put a favorable interpretation on any doubtful statement. In other circumstances, confronting the personnel director with an unacceptable reference would undoubtedly have caused him to back down, considering his duty to keep his company out of trouble.

EXIT INTERVIEWS

Running the gantlet includes an exit interview, and here Arthur made mistakes. He sounded off; and although he felt good about that, the feeling was only transitory. Let's listen in.

INTERVIEWER: They tell me you're leaving us, and I just want to talk to you for a few minutes. Is there anything I can do to help you make the transition to your new employment smooth?

ARTHUR GORDON: It's a little late for that now.

INT: Oh. How were your relations with Ron Smith? You reported to him, didn't you?

AG: He's all right, I guess. But he plays favorites. He makes promises and doesn't keep them. And you can never get a straight answer out of him.

INT: What did you do when you needed an answer and couldn't get one?

AG: I proceeded on my own. You can go all the way up the line looking for answers and never get one. None of those fellows wants to stick his neck out. They all play it safe. So I did whatever I thought was best. I made my own decisions.

INT: Good for you! Did you ever get into trouble over a decision you made?

AG: Sometimes that happened, but I didn't let it worry me. I figured I'd take risks here and see what happened. Then I'd have experience to go on in my next job.

INT: Is that the way the people around you felt—that their jobs were just preparation for going elsewhere?

AG: I can't speak for anyone else, but you get the impression that most people are looking, and that they'd go if they had the chance.

INT: What do you think makes them feel that way?

AG: Let's face it, this company isn't doing them any good. Nobody gives a damn about the people here. Everybody's too busy playing games and taking care of himself. Then they expect supervisors and managers to work late hours just to make them look good. Normal people like to spend some time with their families.

And so on. As the interview proceeded, Arthur created more and more potential problems, should his path cross those of others who may learn what he thinks of them. By contrast, an appropriate exit interview would have obeyed the Law of Self-Interest:

INT: They tell me you're leaving us.

AG: Unfortunately, that's true. It's going to be quite a wrench.

INT: You would have preferred to stay? What went wrong? We hate to see people like you leave us.

AG: There's nothing wrong at all. My associations here have always been pleasant. Ron Smith is a great guy to work for. He taught me a lot that I won't forget. I believe I would have gone far here, if this offer hadn't come along.

INT: I'm sure you would have. By the way, how did you happen to hear of the company you're going with? Did you answer an ad in a newspaper, or talk to an agency, or get in touch with a recruiter? I'm always curious how companies find people like yourself. I like to know what methods are effective.

AG: It all started at a cocktail party, when a friend of mine said that he knew how much I liked my job, so he was reluctant to suggest a change; still he felt a duty as a friend to recommend me for an opening he thought I'd fit perfectly.

INT: So you followed up on that lead?

AG: As a matter of fact, I dropped the whole thing. Never gave it another thought. I told my friend that it would take an awful lot to get me to consider leaving this company and all the great people I've met here. I thought that would be the end of it, and I was very much surprised when they came to me with a tremendous offer. I agonized over it for a long time with my wife, as you can well imagine. In the end, we came to the conclusion that I just couldn't pass up such a wonderful opportunity.

An interviewer who hears slightly modified versions of this story from six different people may come to suspect that at least five of them are pulling his leg, but he will never know which five. There could be no certainty that Arthur was one of them. Meanwhile, Arthur would have gotten across other messages. First, he would have shown that he knew how to handle himself. Second, there would be no point in trying to elicit information from Arthur that anyone in the company could press to his own advantage. If things had not worked out for Arthur in his new job, he might have found a welcome, perhaps at a higher level, with the company he was now leaving. As Arthur actually left matters, the Law of Group Survival would operate to shut him out forever. He had too many harsh things to say about too many members of the in-group who identified the company's interests with their own.

BIG BROTHER

George Roberts understood, in his tenuous position, the need to be circumspect in searching for a new job. He kept his employer's name off his résumé, and he limited his contacts with employment agencies to a select few. He answered only those display ads that carried employers' names. He took great pains to be discreet. Alas, poor George! One agency sent his papers off to an affiliate in another city; the affiliate innocently forwarded the résumé to a local client, which turned out to be a subsidiary of George's employer. Recognizing certain familiar clues, the personnel people at the subsidiary notified their parent company, which, in turn, passed the word to George's boss. For his part, George sensed that something was wrong when his boss began asking how he liked his job. Soon afterward, an understudy appeared on the scene. When someone from headquarters slipped so badly as to indicate that George was known to be unhappy, he realized that his move could not be delayed. The pressure was on.

Companies of all sizes maintain listening posts; and they reward their friends. Those on the outside who cooperate in all manner of projects are treated preferentially when orders are placed and largesse is distributed. If these practices suggest corruption, then rest assured that someone, somewhere will be corruptible. The only real question is whether the company will be first to find such an individual to seduce, or some outside person will be quicker to locate a responsive company operative to deal with. When operatives on both sides profit personally from exchanges involving their organizations, the Law of Aggrandizement is in full force.

From George Roberts's standpoint, the need to be secretive about his intention to leave the company—and about a great many other matters, including his views on a wide range of subjects—imposes limits on his freedom of expression. Outspoken individuals suffer whenever their turn comes to be considered for promotion within their companies, and they get hurt when they want to change jobs. Many less vocal, but equally careless, people are affected similarly. The extent of the harm depends on the effectiveness of corporate antennas in picking up transmissions, weak and strong. This big brother aspect of corporate activity is a serious threat to individuals, because organizational espionage rears its head in many places.

Spying by companies begins at home. *Telephones* invite eavesdropping. In Susan Williams's small company, people listened freely to telephone conversations, until a switchboard was installed. Then the switchboard operators were often too busy to monitor calls, but many people still kept their telephone conversations guarded. Electronic bugging and tapping are reserved for larger operations, and few people are privy to such activities. Although companies are primarily interested in protecting their own secrets, even sophisticated equipment is unable to make discriminating judgments about what is picked up. Those who trustingly reveal their personal secrets and controversial opinions to their companies' telephones are taking chances.

Mail is monitored openly. Susan's boss scanned incoming

mail before it was distributed, looking mainly for customer complaints and other clues that something might be amiss. In companies of medium size, the chore of scanning the mail is often shared by several top officials, with the president merely sampling segments from time to time. In large companies, however, such procedures are cumbersome. Consequently, large company officials are more likely to control outgoing correspondence, which will automatically include answers to problems raised in the incoming mail.

Questionnaires and evaluations are traps. Sooner or later, everyone is invited to complete some kind of evaluation form: How did you like the training program arranged for your benefit? What do you think of certain policies? How do you rate your supervisors? There may or may not be a space for a signature, which is generally optional. The chances are good that everyone whose own standing is affected by the ratings will be able to get his hands on them.

Accordingly, it is best not to turn in an unsigned evaluation. Sign the form, and spare others the trouble of having to analyze handwritings or reach conclusions by a process of elimination. Stand up and be counted, letting everyone know that you can be depended on to say the proper things! Indiscreet remarks, harsh judgments, contentiousness, and overstatement must always be avoided. Signing the form first may help to preserve your defenses as you fill in the blanks. Above all, never allow yourself to be taken in by an unwarranted assumption of anonymity.

Censorship is widely practiced by professional firms. The process starts almost innocently, with a fear that an associate may involve his firm in controversy over a professional matter. Then comes the next, and much more dangerous, step: precluding controversy on social and political matters by requiring that all manuscripts be submitted for approval before delivery to the outside world. It is futile, of course, to try to clear a paper that doesn't conform to the firm's opinion of what may safely be said.

Corporate censorship can also be unconscionable. Employees may be urged, with obvious sincerity, to become active and vocal in political affairs; but those who disagree with the approved line had better disregard such urgings. The tuned-in executive understands the golden quality of silence whenever his inclinations might take him into areas offensive to the upper echelons. The outspoken person's common sense becomes suspect. "How can such a maverick be expected to make sound decisions on company matters," the Establishment's decision-makers reason, "when his thinking is so fuzzy on other issues, and he adheres to his strange opinions with such tenacity? He may be a great guy in lots of ways, and his credentials looked impeccable when we hired him, but his judgment is faulty; and he's stubborn, besides."

The liberal among conservatives and the rightwinger among liberals are not the only ones to suffer for expressing their views freely. Anyone who makes a prediction about anything is begging to have his judgment brought into question subsequently. If a person feels an uncontrollable compulsion to brag about killings on the stock market, he ought at least to wait until the profits are safely tucked away; and he ought not to talk then if his adventures involve wild speculation. Rolling the dice does nothing for his image, even if he makes money at it occasionally.

Psychology is another forbidden subject. Giving voice to behavioral insights brings a reputation as an amateur psychiatrist at best, a suspicious crackpot more likely. In the benighted view of large numbers of people, only a strangely insensitive weirdo would impose on others a disquieting discussion of such things as subconscious motivation. Moreover, ascribing base, unconscious motives to absent persons is only a step away from making similar accusations against those who happen to be present. They have reason to become suspicious.

No matter how guarded or abstract a circumlocution

may be, it necessarily relates to people, and it is often less than flattering, especially in the retelling. An uncomplimentary remark about an individual should not be passed in ordinary circumstances; similarly, *behavioral concepts ought not to induce wandering into forbidden territory, as though it were merely a never-never land of theory, with no relevance to a flesh-and-blood audience.*

Stick to safe subjects—like sports. Even though you may find the vicarious delights of spectator events elusive, you can rapidly glean an adequate supply of information from the sports pages of your daily newspaper. (They're usually near the financial pages.) For your own amusement—not to be shared with others—you can try to unravel the mystery of athletic rites: Wherein lies the attraction to spectator sports? Is it in observing uninhibited competition or in second-guessing the managerial strategies of opposing camps? Is the magnet a reversion to hero worship, dreams of stardom, or exhibitionism? Is it perhaps envy of, or identification with, players who are rewarded by instant recognition of their every achievement? Or do the fans constitute a social group, united in a common cause, with a single focal point for all eyes to concentrate on simultaneously? What's behind the surge in women's athletics, amateur and professional? Such speculation may be no more productive than reading the sports pages, but, for some people, it can be lots more fun.

The foregoing comments on protecting your reputation by discretion may appear to relate only to survival at a current job. However, reputations spread—the bad faster than the good. The business world is a small one, and much information is disseminated through private channels. It is unlikely that you can break away from the past so completely that new associates will be unable to pick up the scent and follow the trail backward. Within an industry, the chances are particularly good that someone in the new company has a source in the old company that can relay a substantial amount of information. Hence, successful jobhunting begins with defensive tactics at your current employer. The traditional job-seeker's gantlet will have to be run, but don't make it unnecessarily cruel for yourself.

By definition, public acts draw more exposure than private conversations, and with long-lasting detriment to careers. Those young people whose naïve faith and sensitivity to injustice encouraged them to peaceably petition their government to end the Vietnam war, or to correct some of the wrongs in our society, must now face this fact: The legal system may have protected them from imprisonment, and the Constitution respects their rights to assembly and freedom of speech, *but* they are not covered by Fair Employment Practice Acts. They have committed no crime, but they will be excluded from certain types of employment, primarily within the military-industrial complex that aroused President Eisenhower's deep concern. Every marcher and demonstrator in the future must be aware that spies will be watching him, long-distance lenses will photograph him, and reports will be filed in his dossier for all time. Statutes of limitation do not apply, and employers' access to those files is not as restricted as it should be. Furthermore, since the business of the typical defense contractor is overwhelmingly consumer-oriented, the exclusive freeze is far more extensive than appears on the surface.

The message is that, in the world of business, the Big Brother era is here—now. While astute observers warn of the evils of big government and the threats of encroachment on individual liberty, government agencies and big business operate an extensive espionage network directed against private citizens. Although it would be incorrect to say that we are living in a police state, it involves no exaggeration to note that essential elements of the machinery are already in place to facilitate further moves in that direction. In addition, people addicted to the police-state mentality know how to find each other, and they can get rough on defectors from their élite corps. Accordingly, any temptation to reveal one's political views in congenial company must be resisted by those who want to further their careers within the organization.

THE CREDIT-CHECK EUPHEMISM

Pandering to the curiosity of employers, a number of seemingly respectable companies actually specialize in digging for dirt. These investigative agencies commonly hide behind *credit-checking* designations, while their dubious activities go far beyond the true credit-checks that local, legitimate credit bureaus perform, mainly for retailers. Undercover investigators may include former FBI and CIA agents on their staffs, side by side with part-time, untrained interviewers who pick up neighborhood gossip, sometimes by telephone canvass, sometimes by personal visit. Police files appear to be rifled by undisclosed means; additional gossip is compiled by snooping among former co-workers.

Susan Williams's company hired a salesperson who had experienced great difficulty in finding a new job, despite good credentials and a warm personality that inspired immediate confidence. His problem stemmed from a "credit-checking" company that had put out a report including a neighbor's observation that this salesperson had been seen at home on afternoons when he should have been working.

The same "credit-checking" company routinely warned its clients never to divulge any of the information provided in confidence. Lawsuits might result! That was before federal legislation required disclosure of an individual's file at his request. Theoretically, a person can now protect herself against malicious reports by requesting the information and the sources of information in her file at any of these credit-checking companies. However, investigatory operations attract employees who are adept at evasion of the law. So it will be some time before a fair assessment can be made of the efficacy of current laws in assuring the accuracy of information disseminated. Lamentably, the individual's right to privacy has long since been stripped away.

Investigative agencies are also required to tell, on request, who has received a report on a person, and recipients must disclose the nature and scope of reports they have requested. Knowing of the unsavory activities of one "credit" company, Susan was determined not to cooperate with employers that encouraged dubious operations by ordering "credit checks." When strange questions appeared on an application for employment, she asked, Why? Why, for example, should a prospective employer want to know her previous address and her address before that? He can't reach her there. Why does he ask about her hobbies and memberships, other than in business and professional associations? Why should she be required to give her husband's name? What are those boxes about separated, divorced, or widowed status doing on the employment form? And whose business is it whether her home is mortgaged or where she banks? Questions like these can have but one purpose: to facilitate snooping into one's private affairs.

IN THE EMPLOY OF GOVERNMENT

No matter who is in charge of a government agency, those who work there have special gantlets to run. First, the sensory apparatus of the sovereign is ubiquitous and inescapable. Second, concepts like loyalty become supercharged with emotion. Third, both practical party politics and the theoretical science of politics impinge on administrative operations and ultimately affect the individual employee. The combined effect of these three influences makes life difficult for people in government.

Government spying on civil servants is pervasive. There is

much concern about government spying on ordinary citizens: dossiers on file, telephone taps, electronic bugs, and investigations that exceed the requirements of law enforcement. The nation cheers defenders of civil liberties and proclaims that vigilance must be maintained in defense of freedom. Then it looks the other way rather than face up to the plight of millions of government workers whose privacy has been invaded routinely for many years. Nobody ever asks why a citizen should be required to give up his right to privacy when he accepts a government appointment. Yet he is investigated beforehand and spied on thereafter by people whose own fundamental beliefs are often legitimately suspect for antidemocratic taint. Nor is the investigating process especially well suited to promote honest, competent government.

Most of the problem centers on mistaken notions of loyalty. In any organization, it is easy for people in authority to identify with the Establishment so closely that their own well-being becomes the system's well-being, and their own ideas and ideology become eternal truths. In government, those who agree with the Establishment are patriots; those who disagree are traitors.

How should the government employee handle himself? The answer depends in part on how he got on the government payroll, for government workers come in two models. First, the careerists are selected under merit-system rules and protected (to some extent) by rights of tenure. Second, the political appointees are either sought out for their views and special competence or rewarded for services rendered to particular parties or candidates; they are generally (but not always) subject to replacement under the spoils system.

Distinctions between merit-system and political appointees are not always clear-cut. The two types of employee can work side by side; political appointees sometimes get themselves covered by civil service rules; and merit-system people can lose their jobs when one office or agency supersedes another, or when retrenchment or chicanery removes their positions from the budget.

Nevertheless, a recognizable distinction does exist. It can properly become the basis for disparate responses to the system. Since political appointees are presumed to adhere to a party and its policies (and to lack tenure, as well), their duty is to advocate, even fight for, the views they hold. Merit-system personnel, on the other hand, may be forgiven for putting continuity of operations—and the saving of their own skins—before self-expression.

5

THE CONSEQUENCES OF COMPANY SIZE

THE WORLD OF organizations likes the neatness associated with labeling; and the labels are made to stick. One of those labels is a size tag reflecting not your own dimensions, but the size of your employer.

Accordingly, company size is important to the individual. Before casting your lot with a company of a given size, it is well to consider the differences between the large and the small. The individual in the small company has greater freedom of action, a broader scope in which to operate and learn. In many small companies—but certainly not all—he may find a shorter wait for promotion, or opportunities to create avenues for his own growth. The large company offers excellent working conditions, including physical plant, systems, and equipment. Co-workers are generally more adept in handling their jobs. Fringe benefits are more attractive. Additionally, there are distinct differences in style. In basic terms, the profit motive operates more crudely in small companies, and in general, more myopically. Finesse and farsightedness are more often found with bigness.

THE SMALL COMPANY

The Law of Aggrandizement operates more boldly in small companies, in part because of loose organizational structure. In the absence of a clear structure, people work at cross purposes. Jurisdictional disputes are frequent—one might almost say constant, because they are seldom resolved.

Preparing your defense in such a situation requires a distinct picture of what exists in the company and what might exist. Since the trouble in a small company begins with individuals wearing several hats and being assigned overlapping duties, the analysis begins with disregarding assigned titles and perceiving *functions* accurately. For instance, when the controller places want ads and screens applicants for jobs in the office, she is performing a personnel function. Meanwhile, if the production manager advertises and screens applicants for plant positions, he, too, is carrying on personnel-related duties. In the absence of a designated personnel manager, a bid by either party to control personnel activities is a fight over no-man's land. A perception of that fact does not automatically resolve the dispute, but it gives one a handle on it. Sometimes the answer lies in creating a new position, bringing in a qualified director to pull together a set of functions that are being performed in many places, and formalizing a consistent set of procedures.

At all times, the relations between people in a small company can be understood best by assigning each, in your own mind, separate titles (and sometimes split titles) for the different hats he wears. For example, organization charts take on an appearance of order, and the actual workings of a company can be interpreted rationally, when the purchasing and receiving functions are separated from the production function, even though the production manager may be responsible for all three.

If one has always worked for small companies, how does

one find out what a properly constructed organization chart looks like? By obtaining one from a large competitor or finding one in a book. The effort is worthwhile, because an ability to visualize clean working relations gives one a decided edge in company politicking.

To anyone who takes the trouble to work out a viable organization plan for a small company, it will become painfully obvious that people willfully exceed their authority. They invade each other's grounds, risking arguments and criticism, partly because, in the end, aggressiveness may help their standings, whereas inaction would not. Criticism is unavoidable either way. "Who told you to do that? It's not what I would have done," is no worse than, "Why didn't you do something about that while I was out? Do I have to do everything myself?"

By contrast, the large company's employees are inclined to define duties narrowly. To be sure, many small decisions are handled according to established procedures. But when written procedures are unclear, or they don't cover a contingency that has arisen, someone will have to make a decision. Each person asks in turn, "Is this decision one that I ought to be making?" The answer they all look for, even strain for, is No. Whether their decisions are right or wrong, decision-makers expose themselves to attack from all sides, as their colleagues belatedly claim prerogatives now denied them. Additionally, there is a good chance that even a reasonable decision will be unfairly blamed for anything that goes wrong.

Worst of all, criticism would be kept from the decision-maker, leaving him no chance to defend himself. To compound his problems, those people who later came to realize that he was right, after all, would continue to distrust his judgment without understanding why; because they had learned a habit and it was reinforced regularly by the attitudes of others around them (not to mention their own self-interest).

Arthur Gordon carried the large-company label, but once he tried to switch in mid-career. Reasoning that he might move up faster in a small company, he set out to explore the minor leagues.

Wherever he went for interviews among the smaller companies in his industry, Arthur's record was much admired, but always with reservations. He was suspected of being too narrow, too much a specialist, even though his experience covered several areas. He was characterized as a typical large-company *nine-to-five* type who would not only exert a bad influence on other employees, but also be hopelessly out of place among executives priding themselves on their dedication to the small companies they had virtually married. This evaluation, too, was unfair, but how could Arthur tell an interviewer that he had always waited until five minutes after his boss left before going home himself? It's especially difficult to say such things in circumstances where the issue isn't raised directly, but a pattern of behavior is tacitly presumed. Nor was Arthur able to convince the smaller companies of his willingness to pitch in and get things done. He was regarded as a person who would carry out assignments meticulously, but who would be unlikely to exercise initiative. Worse still, the smaller companies believed that Arthur would be rigid in establishing procedures and expecting deadlines to be met, and that he would resent suggestions from outside his department as interference. (He probably would.)

Envy of Arthur and his big-company background, along with fear of his potential as a competitor, created opposition to him in many small companies. Over and over, he was asked, "Why would you want to leave a company *that* size?" by people who saw bigness as the answer to all their own problems—bigness to provide security, stability, opportunity, and good living, all at once; bigness with its reflected glory to bask in. Looking at it from the small company's viewpoint, why would a person choose to go small, when he had already been accepted by the leaders and could go on playing in the major leagues? Why indeed!

In time, Arthur Gordon himself began to have second thoughts. The clumsiness of interviewing methods, even the inadequacy of application forms, troubled him. Poor housekeeping in small companies bothered him, too. He wasn't sure he wanted to get used to untidiness. The typical employee of the smaller company dressed, talked, and acted in ways that Arthur found vaguely distasteful. Perhaps he was showing a snobbish or condescending streak, but he was genuinely disturbed anyhow, and to him that was important. Finally, the persistent questioning of his motives for leaving his company—and of his wisdom in wanting to go small— got under his skin. Repeated rejection drove him back to the big leagues. He felt at home, after all, with the larger companies and the large-company types who worked there.

In truth, there was commotion, noise, and wasted effort at Susan Williams's small company. Unnecessary tasks were perpetuated, methods lacked precision, mistakes had to be tracked down and corrected at the source. Humans are social beings, and since these people were too busy to visit socially and their cramped quarters precluded privacy, a steady, general conversation continued almost uninterrupted, with side conversations here and there, as in a social gathering. To be heard, one almost had to shout above the din. Crowding and poor housekeeping contributed to inefficiency, along with antiquated and inadequate equipment, and much time was lost in looking for things that should have been put in their proper place—except that they didn't have a place. The employees in Susan's company seemed to delight in the confusion they created.

A newcomer might enjoy the freedom to say what she liked and dress as she pleased. It all seemed part of a free-wheeling operation in which people could really express themselves. Before long, however, a person was likely to conclude that the small company exercises an oppressiveness of its own. For instance, resistance to change was more open than in large companies. The attitude was plainly, "Why bother to change things?" with a strong hint of "Why bother even to conceal your opposition?" To the typical employee of this small company, noise and bustle seemed to provide a specious feeling that things were happening, life was real, and working was fun. So why be a heretic, complaining that things could be done better and trying to proselytize others, when people were getting along well enough? Who would benefit from improvement, anyhow? Certainly not the "lowly peons" (a term the rank and file affected in referring to themselves).

Top management feared major changes at least as much as the peons. Not knowing in advance what the ramifications of a proposal might bring, and not trusting subordinates to improvise their way out of difficulty—a prudent attitude in the circumstances—Susan's bosses preferred the devil they knew to the devil they didn't, the comfort of the familiar to the turmoil of the new. Meanwhile, the watchful eye of the owner-manager protected him from waste, or so he believed. Impartial observers might have arrived at a contrary conclusion: that while leakage of pennies was slight, a stream of dollar bills drifted down the drain. Furthermore, it was virtually impossible to overturn a bad decision involving the president's ego; the small company's owner can be as frustrating as the large company's system.

EXCELSIOR!

Susan's small company imposed other frustrations, causing her to rebel at the prospect of having to remain forever in the owner's shadow, which was none too long. She was unhappy about having to bargain, cajole, argue, and sometimes threaten before she could squeeze out minimal raises. Weary of the tensions and anxieties that permeated the air, she longed to get away from poorly trained personnel, carelessness, sloppy habits, and lack of concern. In fairness, let it be noted that Susan ran an efficient operation in the midst of near-chaotic conditions, and she performed this feat with negligible support. Against heavy odds, she even found ways to maintain reasonably good morale among her staff. Knowing that she was capable of better things, Susan donned conservative clothes and, with résumé in hand, started the rounds of major companies. Onward and upward—Excelsior!

Beginning with her first contacts, Susan found her patience strained by the formalities of the accomplished procrastinators on the larger companies' staffs. Even as Susan strove to contain herself, she heard her adaptability to discipline being questioned. Interviewers wondered whether she would follow procedures precisely and meet deadlines punctually. Over and over, Susan sensed a vague fear of her presumed casualness, or of a laxity that must inevitably produce lapses and delays. Meanwhile, interviewers suspected that Susan was sensitive, so a tendency developed to bait her and see how much tolerance she had for minor irritations. Poor Susan!

Susan's credentials were also questioned. Big companies gather information about each other quickly and easily, but they have difficulty in evaluating data from less well known operations. Far from being intrigued by the mystery of the unknown, the large-company types view smallness as something akin to disease. What company would choose to remain small if it were capable of unbounded growth? And who would stay with a small company if she had a choice?

Susan's poor reception among the large companies was wholly predictable. At her age—at any age, really—the hierarchical superstructure required that she be brought in at a specific level, and when openings at that level were filled from outside the company, the selection process customarily picked people whose large-company background fit the job with a minimum of perceived risk. Also, large companies tend to conservatism on sexist issues: The thought of bringing in a woman over the heads of nearly qualified males was frightening to men whose acceptance of women's rights did not yet extend to a situation in which male disappointment at being denied a promotion would be exacerbated by gratuitous positioning underneath a modern Lilith.

Where nepotism is rife, prudent people stay away. Only daredevils who are bored with sky-diving should expose themselves to the risks that outsiders face in a family business. When an ordinary person considers joining a one-man show, he ought to find out whether the owner has sons or daughters in school, or whether any other nepotist danger exists. If, after exercising reasonable caution, he is later confronted by a newly developed family situation—the boss marrying a widower with grown children; a hidden son being released from a mental institution—the situation should be viewed with alarm.

Sales is often the safest place for an outsider in a family business. A salesperson develops an outside following, part of which could conceivably follow him to his next job. Whether customers follow a salesperson depends on such intangibles as personal relations and the quality of the products and services of both present and prospective employers. But selling still offers more freedom than management to an individual in a family business. There is often greater safety in making the rounds as a salesperson in the field than in picking up such titles as sales manager. Before agreeing to step up the ladder in a family-held business, it's well to bolster your security with common stock. (The trick is to get some, but more of that later.)

Despite obvious limitations, a small company can become a vehicle for an ambitious employee's rapid progress, owing in part to the owner's seeing himself in competition with other companies—not with his own employees. To be sure, he may think of his business as an extension of himself, and not a separate entity—an attitude that constricts growth. He is likely to be strong in a single field: He may be a top salesman with a loyal following, an excellent production manager, or an inventor. Jealous of his prerogatives, he makes all final decisions of any consequence himself. Furthermore, he generally respects the opinions of outsiders more than those of people on his payroll. He regards exceptional performance as his due; and as he looks to the future, his memory is short. His question is not so much, "What have you done for me lately?" as, "What are you going to do for an encore?" The saving feature for employees (if there is one) is that, although the boss is not overly fond of admitting his limitations, his acquisitive instincts compel him to hire talents that complement his own. With the door thus opened—just a little—a strong employee has a fighting chance to wrest a measure of authority away from the owner. Provided that he is given an incentive.

A small business often resembles a pot-bound plant. A capable person becomes frustrated when his future is narrowly circumscribed. Typically, he finds a loyal cadre of timid followers who have held the show together. These people will never break out of their narrow mold. In their hearts, they fear bigness, and its depersonalization. While such concern is legitimate, it does nothing to promote the company's interest or to encourage the ambitious newcomer.

Along comes Susan Williams, loaded with ideas. Untroubled by her sex, the boss is ready to offer her an executive title. In fact, he is delighted at the prospect of paying less money for more competence, simply because the marketplace makes distinctions that he, in his enlightenment, is free to disregard.

Susan, concealing her resentment of patently unfair treatment, enters negotiations. She must now insist on certain minimum demands. First, she must have a profit-sharing arrangement and stock options. Her stock may never actually become salable to outsiders. No matter. It will have a psychological effect on her boss, and it will provide a measure of protection in the event of a future merger. Susan will also need an appropriate position as a corporate officer, and authority to match. Her prerogatives should be spelled out in some detail, including sufficiently high limits of expenditure she may authorize and areas in which her decisions are final. She must insist on a board of directors that includes outsiders to review important decisions and capital proposals, including those of the president.

This set of arrangements makes sense only for a company which is prepared to move from small to medium size. Only if the owner agrees to such terms can a small company break out of its confines. A capable board of directors and new shareholders can convince the president that the company is more than an extension of himself. It will then be possible to bring in topflight executives in other fields. When these subsequent moves are made, Susan will want to be certain of her own position in the growing organization. Neither expertise nor seniority will protect her adequately. Only contractual rights can be relied on.

Unfortunately for all concerned, Susan's proposal was rejected out of hand. The Laws of Aggrandizement and Power conspired to overcome reason. Like so many self-made people, the owner saw himself in heroic terms—a master who bows to no one's demands. Failing to recognize the Law of Constraints, the boss perceived interdependence as a threat to his sovereignty. Perhaps his horizon was too low. In any case, it was better for Susan to have tested the water —and found it cold—than to have plunged in.

THE GROWTH COMPANY

George Roberts had better luck in his negotiations with a growth company. In this case, the president-and-sole-stockholder had already heeded the call of the outside world. Community activities imposed increasing demands on his time, so the owner engaged consultants, who prescribed a metamorphosis that eventually created an organization capable of handling medium-size, or even large, operations smoothly. Change followed change in wave upon wave of turbulence.

Many things were formalized for the first time. An organization chart was prepared, job specifications written, systems and procedures documented, budgets constructed, and control reports introduced. In truth, the president suffered misgivings at many stages, and it was only when he perceived his own power and wealth being augmented that he accepted the new structure and methodology. But it wasn't easy to watch loyal employees of yesteryear bewildered, frustrated, and hurt by a stream of conversions from personal interaction to impersonal systems. Those who adapted quickly, seizing opportunities to learn new ways, came out ahead—sometimes by taking their knowledge to other companies. Those who rode along, but with no show of enthusiasm, found themselves tolerated—and bypassed. Out-and-out obstructionists were rudely brushed aside. In the end, the president and his new team learned to be comfortable with each other and proud of their organization. In a word, planning, forethought, and scheduling had largely displaced jurisdictional disputes, wasted effort, and recurrent crises by the time George Roberts joined the company.

Still the period of adjustment continued. Further growth, from medium to large size, affected all departments, but at different times. A new plant would create opportunities for engineering, materials-handling, and quality-control people. Increased volumes led to new sales territories and branch offices, and then to additional district offices. Advertising split off into a separate department with executives of its own. Similarly, new departments were created for purchasing, personnel, and research.

Who came out ahead in the years of turmoil? Winners were of several types. First place in their respective spheres went to those who anticipated organizational development and established embryonic staff structures within their own departments. The controller moved unopposed into the title of controller-treasurer, then appointed an assistant controller and, later, an assistant treasurer. Eventually, this controller-treasurer became financial vice president, his two assistants moving up to controller and treasurer. The sales manager, however, concentrated on building his field organization and neglected to build staffs for advertising and promotion. Eventually, a marketing vice president was appointed from outside, and the chagrined sales manager had to report to a newcomer.

Second-place winners were those who latched on to the big winners and stepped up behind them. For the most part, these people had helped to execute the basic strategy, often while they were building secondary, inchoate structures of their own at the lower levels. Thus, when a second plant was built, production manager Johnson made his assistant (by this time) George, the acting manager of Plant Number 1, while Johnson attended to the planning, opening, and running of Plant 2. With his new experience, Johnson was properly poised. The company built more plants, and Johnson became vice president for production. More to the point, Johnson's moves opened opportunities for George to seize. On taking over Plant 1, George Roberts enlarged his purchasing department, so that it could serve both plants. With purchasing under his control, he established his preeminence over plant managers who came later. George became general production manager. Needless to say, both managers had learned to promote their images by graceful fugling.

Some people flourished for a while in the turmoil and then fell into eclipse. When a chief internal auditor was appointed, he reported lapses of such magnitude that he won an enlarged staff to continue the work. Extending the scope of audits brought further recognition of a need for improved systems and cost/benefit analysis. But the internal audit department found itself unable to move into these functions. Systems and planning activities were conducted elsewhere, while internal auditing had difficulty holding its own. Meanwhile, the internal auditors continued to make enemies by uncovering skeletons in the closets of other departments. Eventually, budget-tightening caught up with the internal audit department itself.

Some departments profited from empire-building for a time, only to be found out in the end. An empire-builder must be able to keep his staff busy *and* convince the budget committee that his expenditures have wrought demonstrable benefits. In short, empire-building for its own sake has become risky. While a company is growing, it may seem natural for all its components to expand. Nevertheless, when the day of reckoning comes, an augmented staff must be capable of showing, under the scrutiny of the economizers, that it produces sufficient value to justify its size and outlays. There are safer and better ways for an individual to pursue the Law of Aggrandizement than by building an empire.

SURVIVAL AND SIZE

Company size is a determinant of many factors affecting employees: working conditions, operating style, and upward movement, for example. Moreover, the selection of an employer causes a person to be identified with the company's size as surely as if it were truly one of his or her own characteristics. Furthermore, politicking within a company varies with size and its concomitants: power structure, delegation of authority, new modes of communication, reliance on formal systems, and—usually—separation of management from ownership. Clearly, primary consideration must be accorded the organization's size when you plan your career strategy.

6

GOLIATH

GIANT COMPANIES have been studied by management experts, engineers, economists, sociologists, psychologists, and mathematicians. Occupying a central position in our society, the giants have been fervently denounced and zealously defended. While previously discussing the concomitants of size, we noted, in passing, that bigness in itself tends to discourage initiative. Now it is time to examine other idiosyncrasies of large companies and their consequences for employees.

TALENT-HOARDING

Growth leads to specialization and talent-hoarding. Large operations involve more people, more equipment, more materials, and more money than similar activities undertaken on a smaller scale. Consequently, mistakes—even relatively small mistakes—can be very costly; it pays to have reliable, competent, trained people—in a word, experts—on hand.

Employment of a large number of people also makes it economically feasible to permit specialization. Indeed, large corporations can frequently keep several specialists busy in one limited area.

Obsessed with a nightmare—that there will be no expert available to cover a job—large companies develop a penchant for hoarding talent. Pressure is imposed from on high to recruit more talent than is needed, to train more experts than the company can reasonably absorb, and to build superfluous depth for emergency replacements. As in football, the more depth a team has covering a given position, the less its dependence on the first-stringer; and top management, in sports and business, recognizes the advantages of lessened bargaining strength among the players. The Law of Aggrandizement can operate on all sides.

Recruiting a surplus of talent is not especially difficult for large companies, because they are able to offer blandishments that are all but irresistible. Beginning with a prominent name and comfortable physical surroundings, the typical large company can display its attractive and well-written brochures proclaiming concern for employees (witness the fringe benefits), training programs, support of community activities, and career advancement for ambitious people. Missionaries carry the message to leading universities and graduate schools, while head-hunters are retained to search among the competition.

The selection process grinds along, and the lucky candidates are notified of their success in passing a rigorous screening process. They may now avail themselves of an excellent opportunity to get their careers off to a flying start. Candidates have been transported, dined, and offered an impressive display of hospitality; now they are ready to accept quite a bit of puffing on faith. Still, when newcomers report for work, they find their earlier impressions confirmed. The air-conditioning works; people are courteous; the latest equipment is installed or on order; insurance policies, medical services, and employee activities are not merely available—it would be hard to avoid them. Disillusionment comes later.

The career-bent individual finds much to respect in a large organization. The pieces have been put together by specialists in organization theory and management practice. Methods and procedures have been designed by systems analysts. At every turn, employees are thoroughly qualified for the jobs they perform. Professionalism pervades. Business is conducted in a businesslike way, while social amenities are scrupulously observed. Generally, in-house training programs are prepared and run by experts. But even if there were no formal training programs, the well-run large company would still be a superb on-the-job training school.

Nevertheless, the large company or professional firm can destroy the unwary. Arthur Gordon's academic career had been a long string of successes. Prompted by well-meaning, ambitious parents, he worked hard from the moment he entered school. He won medals, awards, honors, membership in élite societies. Despised by many as an "achiever," he went on to earn a master's degree, pursuing his studies with the same intense drive that typified his previous efforts. After weighing offers of employment from a dozen top corporations and professional firms (proof in itself that Arthur had *presence*—a combination of appearance, dress, grooming, poise, affability, and self-assurance), he selected what seemed to be the most likely vehicle for launching his career—a topflight professional firm. A year later, a sadly disappointed man realized that he was no longer a frontrunner, and after two years, Arthur knew that he could salvage his career only by moving to another company.

What had happened in those two years? Nothing unusual. The firm had hired a number of outstanding candidates, knowing that only one in ten would move upward at a satisfactory pace. Room could be made for two or three others, provided that they were willing to adjust their sights downward. The rest would be expected to leave. Clients of the firm would hire some. The others would be on their own. Arthur had joined the firm anticipating that his service would bring him something more than training, experience, and credentials. Too bad.

It may seem impossible that with a fine academic record, Arthur Gordon could find himself out on a limb within two years on his first job. But education isn't necessarily the key to business success. When Arthur reported for work, he was placed in a competitive situation, which in itself was not unusual for him. His competitors were much like himself: outstanding individuals, intelligent, personable, aggressive, and articulate. Nothing new about that either. However, in the competition that followed, a superabundance of these traits availed no one. What mattered now was a wholly new, unannounced set of abilities: the rubric of *interpersonal relations*, with special emphasis on politicking. Arthur knew how to collect data, marshal logical arguments, and articulate his views. Still, his efforts fell wide of the mark. He wasn't playing the game to win; he wasn't politicking properly. To dwell on his specific shortcomings would be to try to cover the contents of this book in a single chapter. We will not attempt to do that. Instead, we will, throughout the book, follow the experiences of Arthur, George, and Susan in pursuit of their careers. Meanwhile, talent-hoarding by companies has been observed as one of the potholes on the individual's road to survival. It was, in fact, one kind of talent-hoarding that victimized Arthur Gordon.

SPECIALIZATION

A large company showed interest in Susan Williams. With few women in the better jobs, concern for the company image and for compliance with antidiscrimination laws prompted the recruitment of a few qualified female managers. Susan attracted attention with her exceptional credentials, large store of aggressiveness, and good looks, but she lacked specialization. How then could a large company bring her in over the heads of people who understood their jobs better than she did?

Despite the lip-service regularly paid to generalists, it is the specialists who command respect in the large companies. The person who holds himself out as a generalist, without having compiled a successful record in at least one specialty, is looked upon with suspicion by those whose own backgrounds have taught them the value of specialization. The person who has demonstrated ability to handle a specialty before broadening out is not only more likely to succeed as a generalist, but he also has gained superior technical knowledge as a specialist.

At the same time, it must not be forgotten that the most important ingredient of success for specialist and generalist alike is political astuteness. Hence, it is not unreasonable for an individual to move from one category to the other as opportunities present themselves. An opportunity to move into specialization was presented to Susan Williams. After much discussion and negotiation, she was offered a chance to be trained as a specialist in a relatively new and open field —at reduced pay, of course. She would not be coming in over anyone else, after all.

It was now time for Susan to consider the significance of specialization to herself as an individual. The specialist label that the large company was ready to paste on her need not be disastrous. Although some specialties hamper mobility, others can be quite compatible with upward movement. It is often possible to gain exposure and training in several specialties seriatim, so that some people can genuinely assert credentials as multispecialists, with the versatility that the term implies.

Deciding that the advantages of specialization overshadowed its stigmas, Susan accepted the offer.

In time, Susan accumulated the credentials of a specialist: attendance at courses and seminars and appropriate memberships. Moreover, Susan apprenticed with a recognized expert who had been brought in by her company to fill an urgent need. Once the urgency had passed, and Susan was properly trained, it occurred to management that they could save money and recognize Susan's superior abilities by firing the expert.

It took a while for some people to accept a woman as an expert but, having nowhere else to go with certain technical questions, they grew accustomed to calling on Susan. The company encouraged Susan's specialization with a research library and other resources. She had time to think, and occasionally to write. Above all, Susan had the satisfaction of surmounting difficulties and earning the respect of her associates.

The Law of Influence was taking care of Susan Williams. Had she been willing to settle for modest political strength, she could have been comfortable. But Susan was ambitious and wanted prestigious outlets for her talents, and she felt her situation was deteriorating. Despite assurances and vague promises, Susan became aware that there would be no more promotions for her. Since she was needed where she was, a move to another department or division was out of the question, and her specialty was sufficiently narrow to justify precluding advancement in her own division. Although her job was not unique in the industry, her mobility was limited because other companies developed their own experts.

Furthermore, despite Susan's training, she remained a woman in the eyes of management. This last "defect" is unwritten, of course, and its importance is easily exaggerated. Let no man think Susan's predicament couldn't be his own (but probably at a higher salary). The odds on advancement were definitely stacked against her.

Susan's personality altered as a result of her new insecurity. Recruits came regularly with excellent training, equipped to learn Susan's job. No longer convinced of her own indispensability and the company's goodwill toward her, Susan became defensive. Noticeably less communicative, she jealously guarded the secrets of her calling, just as others had thwarted her in the past. Although widely practiced in large companies, these tactics carry dangers of their own. When specialists put their private interests ahead of the company's, they are inviting conflict with management, because harnessing individual effort for the good of the whole is management's highest obligation. Nevertheless, Susan joined the old guard, whose covert defiance of management she not only understood but found admirable. She became cynical about the annual report's "pride in the happy family of employees upon whose efforts the continued success of the company depends."

CONCEALMENT

That Susan Williams was told nothing of consequence, and was left to infer where she really stood, is not unusual. Straight answers are hard to come by, as the Law of Rationalization proclaims. Whether one is being turned down for employment, passed up for promotion, held back from a raise, slandered by a reference, or mistreated in some other way, not only is information being withheld, but the reasons given you are likely to be biased. Companies and their agents do not communicate accurately. In the large company especially, many factors militate for concealment of motives and intentions:

• Self-preservation demands concealment of acts that are unlawful, antisocial, destructive, or injurious to others. Failure to hide such acts invites retribution.

• Creatures of habit routinize procedures and use form letters for recurrent situations. It's more efficient to employ stock answers that work than to respond to each query individually.

• Lazy minds evade thoughtful consideration and careful explanation. Why make the effort to distinguish between people or situations and to comprehend the real motives when plausible excuses will suffice?

• Timorous people refuse responsibility for tipping the company's hand. If honest information given to a prospective victim allows him to rework his plans contrary to the company's expectations, the informant would suffer.

• In fairness, it should be noted that, while protecting themselves or promoting their own interests, people sometimes try to avoid bruising sensitive personalities. Rejection is damaging enough; blunt candor might be unbearable.

Individuals acting on their own behalf also learn to defend themselves by concealing their motives and rationalizing their actions. They are aided by the fact that some aspects of a situation are always obscure and uncertain and subject to many interpretations. Accordingly, it is generally possible to arrive at several explanations of a single set of facts, and to select a particular view that will support one's own strategy and interests.

Before his ascent to the higher levels, George Roberts was considering a promotion that involved a transfer, until the grapevine reported to him that turnover in the proffered job had been extraordinarily high. People had come and gone, careers had been wrecked, and no one had survived. Lacking a venturesome spirit, and instinctively distrusting the motives of those who were engineering this promotion, George felt an emergent need to explore grounds for refusing it. To decline a move could freeze George in his present job permanently. To point to a turnover problem within his company could be dangerous. To object to the management at the new location was inadvisable. Yet a way out did present itself. When George visited the new location for interviews with the people there, he directed his questions at legitimate problem areas that might raise difficulties for him. He came back armed with a dozen requirements for the job that disqualified him without impairing his availability for future promotions that might arise. The Law of Self-Interest was served.

George's analysis went a step further. Recognizing a need to get out of his present position before being faced with any more bad choices, George listened closely to what the grapevine was reporting. Before long, a pending reorganization came to light. There would be an opening—after a while—in a new department of corporate planning, and George could make himself eligible. He enrolled for a course; he read books; and he fraternized with the planners. Admittedly, George's method for choosing a career is not to be recommended for everyone. But he had fugled well; he had gained an opportunity to learn a new field; and he had bought time in which to search for another job, if planning didn't work out for him or for his company.

III

INSIDE THE
ORGANIZATION

7

ORGANIZATION
STRUCTURE
AND THE INDIVIDUAL

THE LITERATURE OF management theory is re-
plete with such terms as *centralization, functional, divisional,
span of control,* and *line and staff*. An understanding of these
concepts and how they work in practice is essential to an
individual's survival strategy.

CENTRALIZATION

When management theorists speak of *centralization,* they
are referring to the degree of control exercised from above.
In a totally centralized organization, the person on top
masterminds the whole show. As an extreme illustration, the
president of a multinational conglomerate was once quoted
in a national magazine as saying, "If I had the eyes, ears,
arms, and legs, I'd do it all myself." Now that's centralization! The obvious inference to be drawn is that executives
in such a company must agree to gather intelligence for the
brain to work with and then mindlessly carry out his orders.

The word that is ordinarily set in opposition to *centralization* is *decentralization*, which is not to be construed as a code word for anarchy. Decentralization is defined in terms of permitting local discretion—provided always that such discretion is directed and monitored from above, in order to ensure conformity to an overall pattern. Clearly, centralization and decentralization are not really opposites, but rather points along a spectrum denoting varying degrees of control from on high.

That the difference between the two terms is relative, rather than absolute, is of fundamental significance. This point explains why, in practice, the actual degree of centralized control depends more on the personalities of executives than on the deliberations of those who draft organization charts. When people disagree, the one who is higher on the chain of command becomes an advocate of centralization, while the subordinate fights for decentralization. If ideas were normally won or lost on their relative merits, then observers wouldn't report dismally high error-rates in executive decision-making. The battles, ostensibly over ideas, are really won by force of personality. The strictures set by the Laws of Power and Group Survival render the theory of centralization irrelevant to the power structure in practice. Like freedom, decentralization must be paid for by eternal vigilance. The price is not too high, considering that centralized control on a grand scale tends to become increasingly impersonal and dehumanized as the *brain* is further and further removed from the functioning parts.

"Why," one may ask, "do companies and, more particularly, government agencies go through the motions of alternately centralizing and decentralizing their activities if the exercise is meaningless?" Such a description denotes centralization in the narrow sense of shifting activities and personnel to headquarters from the field. At times in the federal government, both centralizing and decentralizing have proceeded simultaneously, with truckloads of furniture and files passing each other en route to swapped locations. The reason for all that movement is not to be found in a discussion of the pros and cons of either structure per se. What is accomplished is not operating efficiency, but rather circumvention of tenure rules. An excellently devious way to clean house is to decentralize a previously centralized organization or vice versa. Heads fall in some places while new faces appear elsewhere. Best of all, the decimation can be carried off with a single blow, in an impersonal manner, and for ostensible reasons that give everyone a face-saving out.

FUNCTIONAL V. DIVISIONAL STRUCTURE

In contrast to the superficial debate over centralized *v.* decentralized structure, the distinction between functional and divisional structure can be very real. In a *functional* structure, marketing people report to other marketing people up the line, production people report to production people, financial people report to financial people, and so on. In companies with a *divisional* structure a separate division carries responsibility for each product line, each foreign operation, or perhaps retailing as distinct from manufacturing. Each division has its full complement of production, sales, and accounting personnel reporting to divisional department heads under a vice president.

The degrees of freedom allowed by functional and divisional structures are readily illustrated. In one of Arthur Gordon's employers, a divisional controller reported to a divisional vice president with whom he was in daily contact at their suburban office. This controller explained and interpreted the niceties of accounting theory, the pragmatic effects of alternative accounting policies, and the esoteric content of reports of his department to the division management. By contrast, a plant controller operating within the functional structure of another company might explain the rationale underlying headquarters decrees to local management, but he would have far less freedom of action because he would be constrained by an unending chain of directives from the corporate controller.

There were other differences that affected the personal development of the two controllers under the different organizational structures. The divisional controller met regularly with the divisional heads of production and sales to recommend inventory actions, among other things, to their vice president, who frequently joined their meetings. These contacts between colleagues working together on common problems provided valuable insights into each other's frame of reference. There was no way to gain this not-so-incidental benefit in the field under a functional structure, because policies were established at headquarters and handed down to the local people. Though defenders of the functional structure may inveigh against this tendency, the functional structure lends itself to centralized masterminding.

But beware of easy generalizations! The divisional structure is susceptible to hybridization. When a masterminding attitude takes over at the home office, ways will be found to centralize control, possibly superimposing a functional structure on a divisional one to produce the worst of both worlds, plus a kind of negative synergism. Divisional managers under these conditions are perpetually frustrated by (divisional) provincialism, (functional) remote control, and (synergistic) dual authority, all operating concurrently.

Whatever the structure, in a large organization with many locations, the pace becomes more relaxed as the distance from headquarters increases. A slower pace appeals to many people, but for an ambitious George Roberts, the faster track at headquarters held greater allure. Had he elected to stay with the large company that acquired his small one, either preferring or being reconciled to life in the hinterlands, he might have tried to overcome his disadvantage by arranging frequent trips to the home office, including temporary assignments. He might have fostered a familiarity with people at headquarters, calling them now and again, and spending time with them when they visited his operation.

Those who are employed at headquarters from the start must be aware of a special danger. If executives are prone to boast of their earlier service in the field, that is a bad omen. When such lore dominates the thinking at the top, promotions will be made by bringing in people from field locations to fill headquarters vacancies. In just such a situation, Arthur Gordon spent much time on field assignments, attempting to line himself up for promotion.

SPAN OF CONTROL

Another aspect of organization structure is called the *span of control*, which is simply the number of subordinates reporting to a single boss. Theorists have offered a range of numbers—the number six being typical (shades of Babylonia!)—to encourage efficient operation. If the number six is chosen, then six people report to one supervisor, six supervisors report to one manager, and so on up the line. In theory.

One inconsequential point must be conceded to the number six in a modern setting. In a seven-hour day, a supervisor with six subordinates can meet with each for one hour and still have time to meet with his own manager, also for one hour. That makes for a very neat set of arrangements, if the supervisor has nothing else to do and no one else to meet with, if daily meetings are necessary, and if every meeting requires exactly one hour. Realistically, there are many anomalies. Many tasks are so routine as to require little supervision; it is feasible, for instance, for an entire typing pool to report to a single head. On the other hand, some work can benefit from close collaboration between different levels of management: installation of a system, for example. It is a futile exercise to search for a normative number.

However, left to themselves, managers might opt for too short a span—with disastrous consequences. Assuredly, an individual may find life more pleasant when he has only two assistants to deal with, but if each boss were permitted to structure his activity that way, there would be twelve intermediate levels between top and bottom in an organization of nine thousand people. Compare that with four intermediate levels when the span is six, and consider the oppressive weight of a hierarchy that would compel a request from bottom to top to go through twelve other pairs of hands.

The worst aspect of a short span of control is the opportunity it affords a boss to harass his subordinates. Without enough legitimate work to keep him busy, he is irresistibly tempted to peer over the shoulders of people who are better left to their own devices. Unfortunately, when people are hobbled by close supervision, their dependence increases. In the end, the nagging boss really won't be able to rely on his assistants to act on their own.

Whether the span of control is viewed broadly (in terms of the layers of supervision it creates) or narrowly (in terms of the relations between a boss and his staff), the inescapable conclusion is that *a short span is a diabolical invention which disrupts activities beyond salvage.* The message to individuals is plain: To improve their own chances for survival, they must broaden their span of control by eliminating subordinate *middlemen,* and they must encourage the supervisors who remain under them to do likewise. The Law of Fugling will lend support.

LINE AND STAFF

The line-and-staff concept, borrowed from the military, has created controversy and misunderstanding for many a company. Briefly, the concept distinguishes between adminis-

trators and adjutants, the former being in the line of command, where they exercise authority, while the latter act as
staff assistants with no authority of their own. In business,
the *staff assistant*, or *assistant to*, is perceived as having no
line responsibilities, and he is regarded with suspicion by
those who feel their own responsibilities weighing heavily on
them. As the line people see it, while the outcome of their
decisions and actions becomes the basis for evaluating their
performance, the staff assistant leads a charmed existence,
unscathed by his errors in judgment, as he strews wreckage
in his wake. It isn't really that simple, of course. Staff persons
are evaluated, too, and their mistakes are chalked up against
them. Their main problem is that they operate in a turbulent
atmosphere, highly charged with politics. They are natural
targets, exposed regularly to attack from other staff people
as well as lone operatives. They are frequently resented as
heirs apparent while functioning as the surrogates of executives, despite a paucity of experience. Even while conducting
themselves in the most circumspect manner, many staff assistants find their position almost untenable.

Actually, staff assistants are of several kinds. The one with
extensive background, solid credentials, and obvious ability
has probably been brought in as assistant to the president in
order to acquire perspective and familiarity with the company's operations and personnel before assuming an executive
position. There's no excuse for mistaking such a situation,
or for treating such a person as though he were anything but
an executive. People of this type act self-assured, friendly,
and cooperative; and they ask lots of questions. Don't tell
them too much; don't gossip or criticize; but treat them well.
They are destined not to remain *assistants to* for long.

A second staff assistant on temporary assignment is given
a number of jobs that no one seems to have time for—and
that may or may not need doing. This assistant may also
move into a line position eventually, but the chances are
good that the list of herculean tasks will grow faster than

her ability to handle them. She should be treated like any other person, accepted on her merits, but dealt with cautiously: She does have the boss's ear.

A third staff assistant spells trouble. His chief purpose is to bolster his boss's ego (with cajolery) and security (by reporting rumors). Unfortunately, he can't be trusted to spy honestly. Faced with a dearth of information, he may generate plants of his own and relay to his boss the versions that come back; in ordinary circumstances, he will slant the stories that others plant with him. This type of assistant is easy to spot: He spends an inordinate amount of time in his boss's office; for the rest, he is most often to be seen snooping. Only occasionally will he get a real assignment, which he is likely to foist on someone else. Dealing with assistants of this type is a no-win situation. Being friendly toward them will earn the distrust of others in the company, whereas being unfriendly is provocatively dangerous. Avoidance is virtually impossible, but a pleasantly innocuous stance in casual contacts may work. Above all, the watchword must be "Vigilance!"

A fourth *assistant to* trades on his proximity to the boss, as he hops from person to person and from place to place like an organ-grinder's monkey. At any time, one may find this monkey on one's back, making things difficult, watching every move, perhaps trying to guide the pencil one writes with. The immediate reaction may be to get rid of the pest. However, in working out a strategy, it must be remembered that it's the organ-grinder who calls the tunes. The monkey only dances to them.

These *assistants to*, borrowing authority while being deprived of genuine opportunities to cope with real problems, rarely acquire the confidence to carry off assignments or function in the line at a middle-management level. At any rate, such is the onus borne staff assistants. Consequently, their mobility to the line is limited.

In short, a staff assistant operates in a field planted with land mines. Fugling, development, and consequently survival are most difficult in such circumstances, even for bright young people seeking rapid advancement.

The concept of the staff assistant with all its inefficiencies may be abandoned by management, in favor of a special-services staff. Under such a structure, a requesting department receives competent, professional help, for which it is charged by *transfer billing*. Meanwhile, the special-services staff is kept on its toes by the continual threat that disappointed line people will no longer buy. With perseverance, a little luck, and a flair for showmanship, special-service managers can establish reputations and secure permanence for themselves, provided that they start with clearly defined responsibilities. A highly competent and self-assured person in search of broadening experience and a fast track, and willing to assume heavy risks, might try the special-services route, bearing in mind always the Law of Power, and acting accordingly. However, this route is not recommended for the faint of heart—nor for most other people.

8

DICTATORS AND
THEIR FOLLOWERS

LEADERS COME IN A variety of styles, ranging from
absolute dictators and benevolent despots to constitutional
republicans and deferential democrats. Successful leaders are
not all of one mold. Furthermore, success comes to contrary
styles in disparate circumstances. In some settings, dictators
supplant democrats; at other times, the same dictators hang
by their heels. It behooves a disinterested observer to keep
an open mind about the relative merits of *authoritarian,
democratic,* and *manipulative* styles of leadership in business.

A universal principle of leadership underlies the Laws of
Influence and Constraint: *Interdependence binds leaders and
their followers.* Followers look to their leader for guidance,
but they also assert their own expectations to enjoin his
behavior. A leader can sway his followers on occasion, but he
cannot circumgyrate in matters impinging on their deep
convictions.

Accordingly, *the most important act of an administrator
is the selection of a staff whose philosophy corresponds with
his own.* On acceding to positions of authority, executives

frequently replace subordinates and alter the relative strengths of survivors. The purge is not wrong in itself. What counts is the motive behind it. Incompatibility of leadership style is the soundest of all legitimate reasons for separating people from their jobs. Subordinates need termination as much as the leader. Assuredly, people can adapt to circumstances in varying degrees; nevertheless, a subordinate does himself an injustice when he remains in a group that wants, and has, a style of leadership in conflict with his own needs.

THE AUTHORITARIANS

One style of leadership calls for issuing dictates, enforcing rules, and demanding obedience. This authoritarian style works best with less-educated people performing routine chores, but it also finds willing support among others who fear making wrong decisions. These people criticize, but they don't question. Unable to rebel, they are more likely to develop an irrational pride in contending with adversity and winning personal victories.

When dealing with slavish subordinates, an authoritarian need neither recognize nor cope with individual personality differences. Leniency would be mistaken for weakness. Favoritism rankles among followers, and inconsistency of punishment and reward is resented. In a game of cat-and-mouse, the mouse must lose.

Lest anyone think that the authoritarians are a dying breed, it should be noted that many a political contest is won by nothing more than a demanding style of leadership. "Put yourselves in my hands; follow me; and don't question, because I know best," reflects a political program that millions of people find most attractive. That chilling thought carries over to human behavior in fields outside government.

When Arthur Gordon took over as regional sales manager under an authoritarian top management, he fell in line with its philosophy. Fortunately for Arthur, a set of circumstances conspired to help him centralize control. Each local sales manager had previously run his operation in his own way, more or less by default—a situation top management deplored. Also, a series of disputes developed over the territorial rights of local offices as new communities sprang up, and as old customers opened new branches. Arthur seized these opportunities to hand down decisions and make them stick. One day a report came in that a customer had been quoted different prices by two of the company's sales offices, and all hell broke loose. Arthur saw to that! He followed up immediately, taking full advantage of this stroke of good fortune to impose new controls and tighten up generally.

A few similar opportunities established Arthur firmly in the catbird seat, and he issued instructions that proliferated into a manual. To be sure, at each step, he secured the collaboration of the local managers, who found themselves on uncertain ground. In easy stages, the local people became inured to the new strictures, until their offices were run by the book. From then on, calls to the regional office requested instructions on all sorts of details, many of them quite unimportant, as the local people found it easier to go along with Arthur. Some earnestly came to believe in his wisdom. While local managers played by the rules, they nurtured the hope that they might one day ascend to Arthur's throne. Arthur, however, thought of them as lacking initiative. Operations were uniform and orderly, to the satisfaction of many local people, who felt they had acquired a better idea of what was expected of them.

What can a dissatisfied local manager do to extricate himself from such a situation? Opposing Arthur would invite dismissal. Even covert resistance has its limitations and its risks. A better strategy is to accept Arthur's success and identify the sources of his strength. Does he come up with imaginative approaches? Does he appropriate other people's ideas and make them work? Does he analyze problems well, or know where to get thorough analyses? Does he grasp situations quickly or, pretending to understand, act decisively? Does he rely on business acumen—his own or borrowed? Whatever it is that Arthur is doing right should be of interest to aspiring executives. They can learn by observing and analyzing, while awaiting their turn to move elsewhere. Meanwhile, a suitable strategy combines outward conformity with private second-guessing—all the while testing ideas and methods in small ways, as a prelude to doing bigger things. The situation calls for patience—lots of it.

Among the many people who disliked Arthur Gordon and his high-handed ways, there were some who anxiously awaited a day of reckoning when top management, tired of Arthur's excesses, would depose him. That particular dream was not likely to materialize. Assuredly, another regional manager in Arthur's place might have achieved more impressive results by developing the effectiveness of local managers. But that hypothesis couldn't be tested as long as Arthur's tactics were even moderately successful. He had the advantage of incumbency.

A benevolent despot is welcome to some subordinates and tolerable to others; but *danger lurks in the ease with which a dictatorial stance yields to abuse.* Infantilism, arrogance, secrecy, and deception are among the more common afflictions traceable to virulent authoritarianism.

Any theory that puts emotionalism ahead of rationalism in human relations should be held suspect. The greatest crimes against individuals and nations have been perpetrated by bringing people to a fever pitch of irrationality. Accordingly, an emotional outburst should be treated as an inexcusably degrading act of provocation.

Shouting is seldom encountered in large companies. In that environment, people learn to control infantile tendencies while cultivating more subtle techniques for tormenting their fellows. But in smaller companies, unable to enforce conformity, emotional outbursts are frequent.

There are several ways to deal with tyrannical bosses. Keeping cool is necessary; calmly walking away is acceptable. Sometimes a soft answer turneth away wrath; but soft answers can be highly inflammatory, especially if they are perceived by the autocrat as evidence of superior control. Some people deliberately inflame shouters with silence or gestures, possibly hoping to bring on a stroke. Since the autocrat, in his arrogance, acts disrespectfully, countertactics should be designed for practicality rather than virtue, with this proviso: *never do anything that might cause embarrassment among friends and allies*. Embarrassing a tyrant may be useful if it doesn't tread on the toes of your actual or potential supporters. Extremes should be avoided. A sharp wit may be tempted to ridicule an infantile boss, instead of resigning directly; and that example may win applause. However, in the end, cheap heroics will gain nothing.

The volatile, reactive type with a low flashpoint is worthy of our sympathy. He habitually wins notoriety for belligerence while losing larger political goals of real importance. He characteristically fires off a blast for every inflammatory message he receives. Whenever someone offers bait, he snaps at it; sometimes he seems to welcome excuses for relieving an accumulation of daily frustrations. It may be worthwhile to save some volatile reactors from themselves by encouraging them to compose careful, softly worded, written responses—to be thrown away, of course. A happier method for working off anger is writing barbed verse while the inspiration is strong. Whatever the favored method, it is certainly humane to help another cope with indignities suffered at the hands of a difficult boss.

PERENNIAL NEW BROOMS

The authoritarian mind is characteristically attracted to futile *house-cleaning*. When George Roberts's company was acquired by a larger one, a new administrator was unable to conceive that anyone with tenure antedating his own could be useful. He methodically cut people down, eliminating old jobs while establishing new ones with similar duties, firing incompetents (some of them were), and making it uncomfortable for the old crowd in general. As time went on, however, it became increasingly clear that the new managers were not performing any better than their predecessors had. In fact, some activities were deteriorating. The administrator himself gained substantial experience in the art of conducting interviews, but the company lost ground. A second round of dismissals aggravated a high turnover among new employees, and still the problems persisted.

The plain fact is that the perennial new brooms are genuinely inept in administrative positions. Their problems are further complicated by earning distrust even as they frantically pursue personal loyalty. They meddle in activities and spread confusion among their people, who feel simultaneously undermined below and quashed above.

How does a normal manager avoid a would-be Hercules who thinks he has an Augean stable to cleanse? What telltale symptoms toll a warning? Frequently, certain stock phrases dot the purgers' conversation. When one of them talks about *clearing out the dead wood,* beware! When a prospective boss betrays a cavalier attitude toward his subordinates, know that trouble lies ahead for newcomers, too. The house-cleaners often openly deplore longevity with the company—another bad sign. In addition to these augurs of evil times are the hard facts of high turnover and low morale. It pays to make a strong effort to gain access to such information before joining any company.

In a truly intolerable situation, no counterstrategy will avail. All you can do is shut your mouth, grit your teeth, and look for another job. Just such a hopeless situation obeys a grotesque, but not uncommon, rationale: An arrogant, insecure, erratic administrator demands of his staff, above all else, an unwavering loyalty. Personal loyalty comes to be equated with loyalty to the organization, and under the slogan *pro domino et corporatio*, every sign of unhappiness is interpreted as evidence of disloyalty to the master and his corporation.

Needless to say, in such a situation turnover runs high. When a ritual luncheon is not celebrating a voluntary departure on Friday, the staff waits for the ax to fall on someone less fortunate. Consultants pronounce the company *anxiety-ridden*.

With rampant morale problems, poorly trained personnel, and persistent meddling from above, a self-perpetuating confusion develops. The administrators who cause these situations complain of the incompetence around them, never suspecting their own culpability. To work in such a company is to suffer. There is really no point in joining or staying.

Authoritarian problems originate at the top of the company. Under the Law of Power, these problems flow from the sources of money. Although individual tyrants present an illusion of toughness, self-assurance, and indispensability, in reality they have no more control over their actions than do marionettes. Their façades of intractability crumble in private dealings with their superiors. In fact, the petty tyrants are being used by their autocratic boss to swing the ax on people he wants to get rid of, and to bully employees into working harder. So the local tyrants go on trimming budgets and pounding desks, not for themselves but for their boss. That is either their personal tragedy or their way of making their own sadistic tendencies pay. In any case, other people ought not to submit voluntarily to crude experiments in atavistic management.

DUPLICITY

Susan Williams met up with an inept authoritarian with a penchant for secrecy and deception. His staff complained that he never told them what he really wanted. When a request came down to him, he would pass it along without analyzing it, indicating how to handle it, or even suggesting an approach. Legitimate staff questions were ignored. The response to complaints was glib: "I expect my people to work those things out for themselves. That's what you're getting paid for. If you can't do that, then you ought to turn your job over to someone who can. People who work for me know that they have to produce. I won't hold anyone's hand while he flounders."

Susan found that she got no useful feedback, favorable or unfavorable, on jobs she turned in. "I don't know how a study has been received, or what to do differently next time; and I don't think he's able to tell me, either. He waits to hear what the top brass has to say. Then if criticism comes his way, whether it's fair or not, he gets hysterical. But when a job goes over well, he takes all the credit, as though he had done it himself or directed every step. I'm left guessing most of the time."

While Susan's boss complained that his staff problems resulted from ineffectual recruiting by the personnelists, they responded that he refused to hire people with solid credentials, for fear of being exposed and eventually replaced. He countered that overqualified applicants wouldn't stay, and he continued to find fault with qualified people.

Susan and others were often chagrined to hear themselves misquoted, as their autocratic boss lied his way out of difficulty. Susan often wondered what opinion of her had been circulated by her boss among people at the higher levels of the organization. And well she might wonder! Acceptance of reality is essential in dealing with duplicitous people. They do exist. When you see signs of treachery, believe it! And act accordingly.

Often a person with ideas wonders how many executives in his company know where the credit really belongs. A local boss may be presenting himself as a source of inspiration and a guiding light, so that his staff's successes become his own. What does a subordinate do about that situation?

The answer is: Do nothing. Any direct action will backfire as all other bosses identify with your boss and suspect you of disloyalty. If your boss has really succeeded in getting others to carry him in the past, and they have built a solid reputation for him, then contrary claims will be greeted with disbelief, if not scorn. But if your boss's record was never brilliant before, and it is now, then a newcomer is probably being credited for the change—you may be getting more than your fair share—and it isn't necessary for you to advertise.

The mistake to avoid is underrating a boss in this situation. He may deserve a reputation as an excellent administrator, and he may be seeing to it that his people get full credit for what they do. It's often difficult to find out about such things. For your own good, give your boss the benefit of all doubts. In many ways, the system depends on loyalty, and you don't want to be a renegade—remember the Law of Group Survival. Concentrate on your own standing and progress by making demands and testing your strength regularly. Whenever you insist on a promotion, a raise, or additional perquisites, you are making an issue of your standing in the organization. As long as you keep coming out ahead, you don't have to worry about where your boss stands. He must be doing something right for you.

SURVIVAL

Authoritarians must be expected to abuse their power. In the face of insolence and guile, how do you survive with your dignity and self-respect intact? There is no easy answer. In the end, it may be necessary to find a job elsewhere. Meanwhile, something has to be done until the search succeeds.

In dealing with autocrats, no credence should be given to

their protestations. To hear them tell it, they are the quintessential company loyalists, and they want only to see the very best job done. Assuredly, an autocrat might come to believe that, but dedication to his own career is a far more reliable assumption. The Law of Aggrandizement serves as a commandment to him.

Accordingly, it isn't necessary to make heroic efforts on behalf of the company in order to please a tyrannical boss. He wouldn't be happy if you did! Act tough, push hard (ostensibly for the company), copying the style he has adopted for himself, and he will regard you as a threat to his job. Go your own way, doing your job well and minding your own business; the autocrat will feel threatened by your independence, as though your every move is an act of defiance directed at him. No, these are not valid strategies for survival. An authoritarian prefers to surround himself with people who minister to his suffering ego without endangering his survival.

Manifestly, no self-respecting person is going to transform himself into a sycophant, even if he could. So what is left as an alternative strategy? Try this. Accept (for the time being) the leadership that is there, without questioning its tactics or authority. (The dictator won't tolerate what looks to him like disloyalty, anyway.) Pay lip-service to broad objectives that he enunciates. (He needs reassurance.) Discuss problems with him, for he likes nothing better than to cultivate your personal dependence on him. Take care, however, that the problems you bring him are not beyond his depth. In other words, make sure your actions do not expose his underlying weakness nor threaten his already insecure position. Above all, don't live in hope that another promotion, more money, stock options, or wall plaques will induce new feelings of security and persuade an autocrat to change his ways.

An intriguing prospect is raised by the concept of behavior-modification applied to one's boss. Will conditioning cause a dictator to respond to a pattern of punishment and reward? Using the Law of Influence, it is possible to condition an authoritarian. When an autocratic boss slips out of his pattern momentarily and allows you to participate in making a decision, try rewarding him with an expression of confidence in his leadership, and follow up by demonstrating the effectiveness of a method he has stumbled on accidentally. Perhaps in time, and with your encouragement, he may come to feel the sunshine, even if he never gets to see it. Like Plato's man in the cave, he may find intense light too much for him, but a little warmth is another matter!

You can also use group power and the Law of Constraints to subdue an autocrat. If a boss's behavior is ill-advised, then you might try this tack. Staying with the group, gently educate your associates to expect better treatment. *Gently*, because you don't want to be known as a troublemaker. *Educate*, because you can only point out alternatives; the group must make its own decisions. Perhaps group support can be enlisted in your boss-conditioning project. You can expect better results then, because a leader must accept his group's decisions or suffer the consequences—and these may be dire, indeed. This method is particularly appropriate in establishing the rights of minority groups and women, because others may have similar latent feelings.

Although the prospect of conditioning a boss is beguiling, such a project should be undertaken for its own sake, and not with extravagant expectations. Conditioning may make an authoritarian avoid certain behavior patterns, but it will not instill integrity where there has been none.

9

DEMOCRATIC
LEADERSHIP STYLES

In SHARP CONTRAST to authoritarian leadership stands *participatory management,* in which subordinates are consulted, and they play an active part in the planning process. The participatory method obviously demands responsible subordinates with a comprehension of the objectives and a willingness to cooperate. Creative activities, like research and development, are the ones most likely to benefit from participation, whereas routine operations are the least likely.

PARTICIPATION AND
ITS PROBLEMS

Eventually, Susan Williams's patience was rewarded when a new president projected her into a management position with her own staff of researchers. Remembering her own frustrations, and sensing that creative talent works best when freed from excessive control, Susan permitted her people to follow leads they thought promising. They controlled their own activities, while she kept abreast of progress.

One of the major pitfalls of participatory management is that not all matters need group planning; indeed some issues can suffer from participation. Thus, minor questions of administration can be referred to a professional staff occasionally, but restricting their participation to petty issues would only destroy the morale that democratic methods seek to build. On the other hand, some issues are of such magnitude, or so close to the heart of an administrator, that she insists on exercising her prerogatives. To invite expressions of opinion on such matters, only to disregard the advice that is tendered, would also be destructive of morale. Despite precautions, Susan found that her staff was not always understanding, especially when individuals were disappointed that their own views had not prevailed.

Susan's serenity was disturbed also by another set of problems, stemming from her position as a woman executive. These problems originated with surbordinate women's envy. Since women hold few executive jobs at present, some people casually assume that these few jobs are the only ones open to women, whatever their qualifications. By dint of a giant mental leap, a conclusion is reached that incumbents holding these jobs stand in the way of their sisters everywhere. That kind of thinking may be on the way out, but it dies hard— especially since it is seldom voiced openly, and reason has little chance to prevail. Incidentally, thinking along these lines is by no means feminine. On the contrary, it characterizes all excluded groups, and it derives in every case from an assumption that informal quotas control appointments. How does a woman, or a member of another excluded group, cope with this mentality? An incident from the military will help illustrate a point.

A platoon of officer candidates was lined up. The platoon

leader for the day was calling commands: "Attention. Right shoulder arms. Right face." Now this sequence of commands happens to be in error. The proper order is to turn first, then shoulder arms. The entire platoon knew the proper order, but the general attitude was to save face for the platoon leader, a necessary act of mutual defense within the group, in case an instructor should pass by and observe a leader in trouble. So the platoon faced right—all but one man, who bore a grudge for reasons not altogether irrelevant to this discussion. He stood shouting, "Command! Command!" as a way of indicating his disapproval of the leader's orders. As some of the platoon began to turn back to their original direction, confusion developed rapidly. In the face of this deterioration, the platoon leader had few choices. He could have called out, "As you were," as a way of restoring the status quo ante, and then proceeded from there; but he chose instead to rely on the goodwill of his fellow cadets with a new command, "Forward march!" Confusion ended at once, as a compliant platoon marched off. The recalcitrant member had to decide whether he would conform and march or be left behind. He marched.

The moral of this story is plain enough. When confronted by a recalcitrant subordinate who is ready to undermine your authority, count on the support of the rest of the group—a sense of fair play is deeply ingrained in them—and act decisively. A woman executive, for instance, can exercise her prerogatives as an executive—not as a woman—and she will be treated accordingly. Let her motto be, "Forward march!" as she relies on her associates, and she will leave the snipers behind. *Most people are fair, they want decisive action, and they are carried along by a winner.*

Unfortunately, Susan discovered yet another, more intractable problem inhering in participatory management itself. A manager must assume a posture of dedication to the company's aims, which are presumed to find their highest expression in the policies of top management. Opposition is not tolerated. At best, disagreement with management will be rewarded with disapproval that is likely to become personal.

Management's long-range corporate plans preempt all others. Long-range forecasts are generally conceded to be nebulous—the further out they go, the less reliable they become. Yet sophisticated managements commit their companies to long-range projections, requiring that short-term plans conform to long-term, and further, that divisional and departmental plans adhere to general corporate policies. Moreover, individual schedules are expected to conform to departmental projections. An individual may try for departmental modifications, but blatant opposition exposes him to unnecessary, and fruitless, risks.

Then where does participatory management enter? Actually, *participation in management decision-making is untenable.* The individual can be invited to make decisions only so far as they are congruent with preordained goals— and they commit him to a standard for evaluating his own performance. The process is more accurately described as *involvement* instead of participation. (It has also been known as *management by objectives, MBO;* and that term has suffered setbacks, as people began to penetrate the veil of deception.) While individuals are expected to become involved, true participation is not altogether welcome. Involvement, yes; commitment, yes; real participation, maybe. Under such conditions, commitment to objectives, plans, and standards—even "voluntary" commitment—is viewed as a trap by the perceptive people that participation is designed to captivate.

Consequently, Susan has become wary. She shows her staff the limitations imposed on her, so that, knowing the ground rules, they may alter their expectations. Even so, their frustration can create additional problems for Susan to cope with. Participation has real drawbacks when genuine alternatives challenge the Establishment's position.

BALKY SUBORDINATES

No matter what style of leadership you practice, an inherited subordinate may offer resistance. The only time such obstinacy creates a dilemma is when a manager and her company espouse a democratic, participatory style, and the supervisory subordinate is authoritarian to the marrow. How can the manager, in good conscience, direct the manner in which a supervisor must handle his relations with his staff, when the manager is committed to encouraging self-actualization for all? The recalcitrant supervisor may be sent to courses in the behavioral aspects of management, but she can't be forced to alter her habits.

To ignore the situation would be to deny the staff the type of leadership the company has ordained. Yet forcing the supervisor into a prescribed mold is an act contrary to the leadership the manager, enlightened by her company's established policy, can offer. By her rationale, compulsion won't work.

The solution to this dilemma lies in the concept that different people need different kinds of leadership. Accordingly, the first question to ask is, "What kind of leadership does this supervisor's staff want?" If the work attracts authoritarian types, don't meddle. Let him be. Whatever the kind of work, if the staff is performing well, tread carefully: Don't move until symptoms of discontent appear. Meanwhile keep a watchful eye on the situation; don't sit by while good people are driven out. In short, only when a supervisor's problems surface can his boss afford to intrude. High turnover is one such problem; absenteeism is another; poor quality of output is a third.

When the time comes to take an autocratic supervisor in hand, act promptly. Take a firm and dictatorial stand with him. That kind of treatment is, after all, what he understands, respects, and wants. Order him around. Listen to complaints from his staff—this would be doubtful advice under other circumstances—and confront him with his problems. If his conduct is destroying him as a leader, you will be helping him to survive.

In the end, the hope is to give the democratic types on the tyrannical supervisor's staff an environment they can live with. Don't worry excessively about the authoritarian types on his staff. They will respect a manager who is dictatorial toward their supervisor. You can afford to be absolutely intolerant of every move that affronts the democratically oriented. Ride the tyrant hard, and pull him in tighter every time he strains to get out of line. Show him that you can be as tough as he is.

In acting tough, you will learn something else: the stern postures are favored by authoritarians because rigidity offers an easy "solution" to problems. When a person is rigid, he doesn't have to think, and he needn't choose between alternatives. When you discover how easy it is to deal with a dictatorial subordinate by acting tough, you may learn to love him, even though you will never respect him.

In short, the problem of the authoritarian subordinate need not be an insoluble dilemma. It is essentially a practical problem between people, to be worked out realistically. The autocrat may appear to suffer under harsh treatment, but he's asking for just that sort of leadership style, and he probably thrives on it. Perhaps there ought to be a Silver Rule: *Do unto others as they want to be done unto.* This new rule may not match the elegance of the venerable Golden Rule, but it has its place in management.

THE GROUP

In favorable circumstances, participation has a better chance of working under a style of leadership that makes use of a ubiquitous social entity, the group. George Roberts has observed that the head of the maintenance crew consults with his lead people before announcing decisions, and he permits them to establish their own standards. On their side, the crew is obviously loyal to its manager. The group displays a pride of workmanship and a strong, perhaps exaggerated, sense of responsibility for keeping the plant in operation. Standards are enforced promptly against wayward members, and individuals are expected to turn in their best effort. Stalling on the job is something the group feels it can detect, and it disapproves. At the same time, the group insists that its members break promptly for meals and rest periods, and the group arranges informally to equalize overtime among its members. Although the manager assigns people to jobs, he consults beforehand with his lead persons. His scheduling and reporting paraphernalia are open for his crew to see.

Groups form naturally, and they exert a powerful influence, for good or bad. Tyrannical group pressures on an individual can become unbearable. To use a group as a vehicle for personal leadership requires open communication with the group and an alertness to their needs. The maintenance manager in George's company had been his group's natural leader before his promotion. More articulate than the others, he had become their spokesman, and continuance of their loyalty strengthened his hand.

Groups can be treacherous. Internal discord can become a snare; and a group can march off in a divergent direction, deserting their former leader. In short, group leadership can be effective and rewarding, but also very trying.

An individual works in a local pyramid typically comprising a boss at the top, peers in the middle, and subordinates at the base. The large pyramid that is the company contains many such small pyramids, and pyramids within pyramids. A middle-management person at the apex of one pyramid can be in the middle of another and at the base of a third.

As you reach upward in pursuit of a career, your friendly peers and co-workers in a local pyramid are the people most likely to hold you back. They perceive you to be in direct competition with themselves, and they don't want you to raise the standards by which they are judged. If you show more interest in your work, or bring more talent to it, you will hear such accusatory phrases as *bucking for promotion.* And if you should be promoted, they will constantly remind you that they *knew you when.* If you get on the wrong side of your co-workers, they may withhold information, exclude you from their pipeline, and perhaps go out of their way to make you uncomfortable. The group can be influential with the boss, labeling you as a *loner* who doesn't get along with others; the consequences to your career can be disastrous. After all, your boss is their boss, and the Law of Constraints affirms that he needs their cooperation.

How does one beat that game? First, despite all provocation, stay with the group and observe its rules. Don't go off on your own (unless you elect to be an innovator—as we shall see). The road to recognition need not include doing better or faster the same things that others do. Try for informal leadership among your peers. Rule out local attention-getting devices and oneupmanship within your pyramid. The group will be quick to notice and slow to forgive. Second, maintain good relations with the boss, but don't fawn over him. Keep the lines of communication open; discuss issues, ask advice, provide answers to questions, handle emergencies, show an interest in his pyramid's activities, but don't look too eager, and don't be obsequious. Third, make contacts elsewhere in the company. A break may come from another department.

If an opportunity does come to move to another pyramid, you will be glad that you have a good record as a team player, because the new pyramid will be as demanding as the old in its insistence on rigorous conformity to group codes. As you move up the pyramidal structure, the conquest of each level will cause you to be looked upon generally as a stronger, more successful, and therefore more dangerous competitor.

At the same time, each new level puts you in competition with others whose progress matches your own. Through all of these moves, it is most important to leave a good trail behind.

For a woman among men, some avenues are virtually closed. Gaining acceptance in an all-male group is a major hurdle. Even having lunch with some male members may prove impossible. Striving for leadership is unrealistic, unless the group is quite intellectual. However, changes in the composition of the group may make it mixed—perhaps balanced between the sexes—in time. Meanwhile, the avenues of innovation and outside contacts are available for the ambitious woman.

There are advantages to moving upward in a different pyramid, location, department, or company. To be sure, the people around you in the new assignment will have to adjust to the stranger in their midst—just as you will have to adjust to them—but they won't be troubled by remembrances of working shoulder-to-shoulder with you. The new person comes among them as a full-blown manager, as though born to a superior station in life. In that respect, the transition is easier.

INTERACTIVE LEADERSHIP

Among behavioral theorists, participative management is given high marks, and group leadership is greatly respected, but *manipulative management* is scorned as a perversion of democratic doctrine. However, from a pragmatic standpoint, manipulation is practiced widely and effectively. Skilled users of the manipulative technique have refined it to a state of elegance deserving of a less pejorative designation. As an aid to shedding prejudices, a name change is in order. *Interactive management,* a term not burdened with derogatory connotations, is more descriptive of the true nature of this leadership style.

The interactive leader is aware of individual personality differences and considerate of other people's feelings. He treats people as individuals. Rather than issuing autocratic orders, he asks his subordinates for their advice and leads them around to his way of thinking. When the time comes for disciplinary action, or even a mild rebuke, he talks quietly, privately, and with understanding. He still believes the *sandwich* has its place: putting criticism into the middle of a conversation, preceded and followed by honest praise for accomplishments. He knows praise is reassuring to people in a stressful situation.

In other circumstances—for instance, when a dispute arises—the interactive leader is less interested in rights and wrongs than in compromise and reconciliation. He devotes considerable energy to seeing that people get along, and that they work together in harmony.

Others may object that these harmonious relations are superficial, and that resentments simmer underneath. The answer would be simple: "Smile and you will be happy. Act friendly toward others, and you will begin to feel friendly toward them, especially when you get a friendly response." It doesn't trouble an interactive leader to reflect that an inordinate amount of his energy is dissipated in meeting the needs of others. That's the nature of his job; and by catering to other people, he gets his own way in the end—in fairly pleasant circumstances, at that.

An interactive leader scoffs at the charge of manipulation. When he plants an idea in someone else's head, is he really fooling that person—is that manipulation? In his view, he is giving the other person the satisfaction of coming up with an idea and seeing it through to completion (with encouragement, besides!). If that is fooling people, then perhaps they rather like to be "fooled" that way. The interactive leader develops people's self-confidence and self-respect. Since he asks nothing more for himself in his dealings with his own boss, he feels justified in looking upon himself as a practitioner of the Golden Rule.

There is, of course, much more to the interactive mode of operating than one-to-one dealings with people. The interactive manager keeps in touch with de facto group leaders in his department. Viewing group influence as the chief potential rival to his own authority, he characteristically identifies and cultivates the natural leaders in the groups he deals with, even as he works with the formally appointed supervisors.

The activities of the interactive leader in business parallel the operations of a professional politician: seeking out local leaders within his party; keeping these leaders informed; listening to them; explaining positions, especially to those who may hold opposing views; working out compromises; *doing favors*; and spreading the perception that all are participating, *through him*, in the operations of government. Obviously, no politician can please everyone; some differences are irreconcilable. But *a good politician makes his constituents feel that they count for something.* If you hanker after party politics—which is to say, a steady diet of placating, mollifying, and attempting to win over dissident constituents —you ought to consider applying the same tactics in business, where the game is not so demanding. The risks are lower, in the sense that recurring all-or-nothing elections are not mandatory; and you'll probably fare better in business than in politics—financially, at least.

THE LEADER AND HIS LIEUTENANTS

Successful leaders can be found making many different leadership styles work for them. If there is one point essential to an understanding of leadership, it is the fundamental importance of followers to their leaders. That is the sine qua non of leadership, and the basis of the Laws of Influence and Constraints.

The task of holding the followers in line often falls to subleaders and lieutenants. Accordingly, *the leader must adopt strategies for tying his chosen lieutenants to himself, and for bolstering their efforts in his behalf.* He or she must see to it that lieutenants receive the recognition that is their due, that they are granted perquisites and titles, and that they have authority to act on their own. Of the many reasons for delegating authority to the lieutenants, the most important is that they can function more effectively if they have visibility, prestige, and the respect of the rank and file. Second, the leader who takes pains to establish his lieutenants' credentials in their own right looks good himself. Third, the leader who looks after his lieutenants, sharing with them the triumphs and the publicity, can expect to generate enthusiasm among his following in return. Moreover, the leader who looks after his lieutenants, according them privileges, puts himself in a better position to demand loyalty and to withhold recognition from those who stray.

To be sure, the lieutenant who has acquired credentials of his own may one day bolt to the opposition. That risk must be taken. Too many leaders egotistically hog all the glory themselves. The temptation is great, and an exaggerated need for glory may be what prompts some people to seek power and influence in the first place. Nevertheless, the Law of Fugling requires that such temptation be resisted; a leader can do better by supporting his lieutenants while they support him. That principle of mutuality holds true in politics, in business, and everywhere else.

IV

POLITICKING
FOR
SURVIVAL

10

POSTURES
AND STRATEGIES

T H E R E   A R E four basic postures an individual can assume
in politicking: loyalty to a leader, loyalty to a group, independence of others, or dissidence. Since party politics is considered newsworthy, whereas business politicking, mercifully,
is not, followers of the news media have had great opportunities to watch political stratagems, while opportunities to
observe business counterparts are normally limited. This
chapter will draw illustrations from both business and party
politics. Regardless of source, however, the conclusions are
universally applicable.

RIDING A COATTAIL

In party politics, when the top of the ticket is expected
to win by a very large vote, other candidates of his party
seek election by *riding on the leader's coattails*, identifying
with his record and platform. Similarly, in business, when an
executive moves upward, he frequently carries with him a

loyal band of cronies. Aspiring managers often look for a star to hitch their wagons to. Obviously, selection of a genuine star in its ascendancy is most important.

George Roberts was generally content with his new company, but he wanted a faster track. When he realized a particular executive was headed for bigger things, George began maneuvering. He clipped news items and magazine articles relating to the star's field, and he delivered them in person. "Just thought you might be interested in this item." "I'm sure you know about this matter, but here's a view that's a little different from the usual reporting." "What's your opinion of this suggestion? Is there anything to it? I respect your views." George improvised a number of gambits.

As a next step, George looked for his star at meetings and social gatherings. In the company cafeteria, he stopped to exchange pleasantries or chat awhile. Careful not to overdo what was intended as a subtle pitch, George limited each meeting. Watchful of signs of impatience, he preferred to bow out too soon, rather than risk becoming a nuisance. Meanwhile, George picked up information on his star's outside interests. George began to make regular appearances at a local bar, not to barge in on gatherings there, but merely to say hello to the executive and to find out who his cronies were. By paying a little attention to these friends whenever he could, George speeded up the process of acceptance in the group. Thus, step by step, he developed closer ties with an in-group. The campaign paid off when George was offered a promotion to his star's division, and a chance to work closely with him.

Arthur Gordon didn't have to find a star. His position gave him access to the president. When the company moved Arthur to its headquarters, he found that realtors who showed company personnel around had marked the residences of important persons on their maps. Arthur selected his house with politics in mind. After moving in, he chose his transportation the same way—taking the same train as the president morning and evening. This practice stretched Arthur's working day, but it gave him the president's ear for an hour and a half, uninterrupted by telephone calls. Think how many axes can be ground in that time!

The Gordons lost no time in socializing with the boss. Not ones to wait for the first invitation, they held a house-warming party. Later there was a group from the office, then a special occasion. When the president's wife reciprocated with an invitation to a cocktail hour, the Gordons rejoiced; and they followed up promptly.

Clearly, this method of career advancement is not for everyone, but there are those who seize such opportunities when they arise.

While holding the posture of loyalty to a leader, it is one thing for a person to cultivate his boss, especially if common interests provide a reason. It's something else again to be a yes-man. Far removed from graceful fugling, toadying earns contempt.

Susan Williams was treated to a show of the sycophant's art that she won't soon forget. Arriving early for a meeting in her boss's office, Susan found the fair-haired boy of the office already there, trying to pick up clues to the boss's leanings.

When the meeting opened, a problem as momentous as this was thrown out: "Strangers have been found wandering about the building. Small items of personal property have been missing. Some of our employees have lost money. So we are taking measures to tighten our security. For one thing, the reception desk will be covered at all times, and no visitor will be allowed to pass without an escort to take him where his business is to be conducted. Now someone has proposed that, in addition to these precautions, we lock both the men's and the ladies' rooms. What do you people think? First, are there any questions?"

There were indeed questions, as those in attendance tried unsuccessfully to elicit important pieces of information:

What further suggestions had been made, and by whom? Where did the boss stand in all this? Finally, individuals were called on for their opinions.

The first four people were evenly divided on the issue. The next speaker was in favor of locking just the ladies' room.

Now it was the fair-haired boy's turn. In a deep, rich voice, he intoned, "I can see why this is a problem. There's more to this issue than meets the eye. I wouldn't want to be too hasty to say Yes or No, or even, as someone here has suggested, Yes and No. The situation should be thoroughly examined in all its ramifications, and every aspect should be carefully explored. It's better to take a little time now to work out a completely satisfactory solution than to have to reconsider later, perhaps with egg on our faces as we reverse our own decision.

"I must say that the preventive measures you are taking look mighty thorough to me. You've thought of everything. Still, we must allow for the possibility that a professional burglar, by some ruse, perhaps with an accomplice to distract the receptionist, might be able to get into the building and up to our floor. Unlikely perhaps, but conceivable. At this point, he looks for a temporary hiding place before making his next move. The rest rooms would be his first choice. They're conveniently located. Anyone in a rest room would be exposed to the danger of having his or her wallet stolen, and perhaps also of being assaulted physically.

"These are very real possibilities, and yet I can see another side, too. It may be that nothing of the sort I have described would ever happen. In that case, if we installed locks, there would be unnecessary expense and a great deal of inconvenience. I'm afraid I need more time to think this over. In my judgment, this is just too important an issue to be decided hastily. Both sides obviously have something to say and conceivably, they may both be right. So I'd like to pass for the time being, and I would appreciate it if you would come back to me later, when I've had a chance to sort out the facts in my own mind and really think the problem through."

"I've had trouble with this one myself," said the boss, with evident pride in his boy. "Take your time. We'll get back to you later. Susan, how about you?"

Following the fair-haired boy's lengthy discourse, Susan and later speakers felt a need to talk longer than they might have otherwise. Accordingly, Susan acknowledged the gravity of the decision to be made; she deplored the circumstances that had led to it; and she added whatever other observations she could. Susan concluded that it would be discriminatory to lock either the men's room or the ladies' room while leaving the other unlocked.

After giving everyone a chance to speak, the boss summarized the arguments pro and con, and he announced his decision: "I am persuaded that we should lock both rest rooms."

Without a moment's hesitation, a single deep, rich voice boomed a resounding "Yes!" But while the boss felt reassured, others in the room were contemptuous. Therein lies a problem for all sycophants—and for bosses whose egos respond to flattery. They don't look too good, either.

The follower syndrome may take other forms among individuals who select a star early and remain in his shadow. Sometimes self-effacement becomes so strong a habit that, after the strategy succeeds, the new manager finds it impossible to rely on his own resources. He may then timorously turn to his subordinates for much more support than custom condones, relying unwisely on their judgment and discretion in keeping his secret.

Since the successful executive normally exudes self-confidence, the timorous manager is something of a freak, like the cowardly lion. Getting along with him, in a subordinate role, involves catering to his needs without threatening his security. The real problem in being stuck behind such a manager is that he seldom reaches the highest levels. A secondary problem arises when his judgment is held suspect in

the higher echelons, so that even the subordinates he favors
don't fare especially well.

PLAYING ON THE TEAM

A generally safe strategy is to play on a team; except that
the existence of competing teams may cause recurrent selection problems. As everyone in politics of any sort knows, the
team to join is the one that's going to win. There are no
rewards for losers. Yet there are two opposing practices, even
in such an obvious matter as this. On the one hand, openness in picking a winner is denounced by some as opportunism, so that rationalization is a frequent recourse. On the
other hand, there are people who feel no qualms at making
such forthright declarations as, "I'm with them because they
can win." Nevertheless, an excess of candor on this score
does appear gauche to many people.

Among old-line politicians, the team is everything, and
team players are the only *good people*. The Law of Group
Survival is supreme. The *regulars* who hold appointive government positions are always ready to round up volunteers,
raise money, and look after the interests of the party and its
candidates. Ask a favor, and they generally oblige. But they
attach a condition, expressed or implied. When they're selling tickets to a ball, for example, they expect their friends
to take handfuls. Turn them down and there will be no more
favors. They may even go so far as to look for ways to take
back old favors. Teamwork involves a recognition of obliga-
tions incurred. "One hand washes the other." "You scratch
my back, and I'll scratch yours." When Susan entered party
politics, the old clichés acquired a new vividness for her.
Reciprocity was the order of the day.

There are certain caveats in team play. Where there are
warring factions, some people will change sides from time
to time. Players come and go; even the reasons for staying

with a particular team, or leaving it, may change. Today's ally may be tomorrow's foe, and vice versa. Accordingly, when there is dirty work to be done—something that will hurt the opposition—Susan leaves it for someone else. Hatchet-wielders create enmities. Those who steer clear of such activities are more likely to retain respect, and their heads.

Not only does Susan duck away from assignments that will cause someone to lose a job, miss a plum, or suffer embarrassment, but she scrupulously avoids recommending or planning such plays. When she changes sides in a party split, she manages to keep the lines open to her former associates, and she deals straight with them. With one eye on her own team, and the other watching the opposition group from a distance, Susan maintains contact with a large number of people on both sides.

Is it possible to stay out of conflicts by remaining aloof? Not for long. Remember the fable of the bat in the war between the animals and the birds. When the animals sent a delegation to enlist his aid, he spread his wings; but then he told the birds he was a mammal. When hostilities ended and the two sides were reconciled, the bat found that his neutrality had earned him the status of a pariah in both camps. So it often is in party politics, and in company politicking, too. There's no escape.

That's how George Roberts sees it. In party politics, he is always climbing on bandwagons, and he understands the value of careful timing. When a new favorite looms on the horizon, George is cautious about jumping into his camp too soon. Not only is there a possibility of gross error, but there are also matters of delicacy to be observed in leaving people behind. The first to move out of the old camp may be long remembered for their treachery. So George bides his time.

He can't afford to wait too long, of course, because laggards will be regarded as outsiders by a new régime. Consequently, George goes through a series of stages. He expresses disappointment here and there at the way things have been managed or the failure to attain results. Then comes a time of disenchantment, followed by a period of independence from both sides. While George is thus making up his mind, overtures come from the new camp, and he cautiously leans toward their position for a while before finally announcing that he is joining up—for reasons that follow the Law of Self-Interest.

In this simplified version, the negotiating over prerogatives and prospective spoils has been overlooked in order to make the single point that matters: diplomacy cannot be rushed. George wouldn't think of sneaking over to the other side. Nor would he approach them with hat in hand, asking favors. Protocol must be observed; mutual respect must be upheld. *Natura non facit saltum,* "nature does not leap"; and fugling must accord with nature.

INDEPENDENCE

Not everyone agrees with George Roberts's assessment of the futility of an independent stance. Some individualists believe in hacking their way through the wilderness, maintaining contact with opposing camps, but never identifying with one or the other. Neither rebellious nor defiant, they seek alternatives within the existing framework. Sometimes the posture works despite repeated attempts on all sides to draw the individualist into squabbles and force him to take sides. The true individualist stands like a rock in the midst of swirling currents—until he's dislodged. To avoid discomfiture, he must not forget the Law of Power—PFM—in seeking support and establishing himself as a force to be reckoned with.

Realizing that he will be called upon frequently to justify his independent conduct—which may include faits accomplis or forays into others' territory—the individualist needs to keep his defensive plans in a state of readiness. Timing often falls to the opponents, who are free to seize the initiative at will; but the individualist can prepare for a conflict by designing specific defenses and lining up support in advance.

Although an individualist may occasionally dream of a personal following, he would probably be uncomfortable with the strictures imposed by the Law of Constraints. In any case, it is unlikely that that particular dream will materialize. The independent steps on toes too often, breaks rules, is unpredictable; and so his successes arouse resentment. He can seldom expect to reach the pinnacle, but he can have a unique standing in the company: respected, envied, and vaguely feared. Some think of him as a maverick (which he is); and others think of him as a free spirit, bent on the pursuit of his own follies, obeying his own dictates, and dangerous to all around him. All things considered, he could have a better time at his job than his associates, which is an accomplishment in itself. But while operating under the Law of Influence, he must be careful not to run afoul of the Law of Group Survival.

A research manager in George's company disputes the usefulness of feasibility studies to evaluate the relative potential of proposed projects. Asserting his individuality and freedom, he is fond of saying that feasibility studies look great on paper, but that's all. "You do a partial study and reach a go/no-go point. If the word is go, then you continue until you arrive at a second decision point. If the word is still go, you continue on to a third and fourth; and when you're finished with the study, you know how to proceed. But the fact is that such rigid methods are not valid for judging original ideas. At best, those decision points and criteria are like road maps—good as long as you remain on the highways, but once you take to the wilderness, you're on your own. Try telling that to the ordinary consultant!"

This manager with an independent turn of mind goes on, "A feasibility study for justifying an allocation of funds to a proposed project is a sop to a committee with no imagination and no guts. The committee members want neat reports, nicely bound. Something to look at and to get them off the hook. In case of failure—and some projects are bound to fail—they can always say afterward that they acted prudently at the time, but the report misled them; or something to that effect. To my mind, the whole charade is a waste of time."

As to the value of the conclusions reached by feasibility studies, this manager has more to say: "Some of our most successful projects would have been consigned to the junk heap if I had listened to the opinionated self-styled experts. In fact, I sometimes think that the way to get the jump on competitors is to deliberately ignore conventional wisdom, and even run counter to it." Some people have indeed prospered with precisely that strategy.

A friend of Susan Williams is an independent operator of a different, and more opportunistic, sort. She specializes in rescuing projects that appear to be floundering. Originally, Diana had done quite a bit of trouble-shooting for the company. Since her successes had gone unnoticed—except by the people immediately involved, who frequently stole the credit —she adopted a new strategy. Before straightening out another project, she insisted on taking it over. (It was easy pickings, then.)

Accused of having moved in on activities that were nearing the end of their initial trials, when improvement was imminent, Diana replies, "If anyone has a schedule that he intends to meet, then he's a fool not to let his boss and everyone else know that he is making progress, that he's living up to his schedule, and that he's going to get the job done on time. If progress is not evident, then others are entitled to assume that things are not going well. People who are doing their jobs well shouldn't leave themselves exposed."

Independents are difficult to deal with, mainly because they want to be. As in all contests, a suitable defense must reckon with the particular independent's strength. If he is cognizant of the Law of Power, and he has built solid support or real influence among the sources of funds, discretion requires recognizing his exceptional merit and working with him as well as one can, never forgetting his proclivity for turning away from his friends and taking off in new directions. But if the independent lacks support, then it is appropriate for others to stand aside. There will be people conscientiously dedicating themselves to the cause of bringing down this independent, and they will heap enough blame on him that the excess could easily tarnish the reputations of innocents close by.

Essentially, independents separate from the pack in the hope of creating an aura of individuality about themselves. Ultimately, they look to this aura to free them of the operation of the Law of Constraints. In pursuing this dangerous course, independents are often guilty of infractions of the Natural Laws of Organizations. Hence they must accept recurrent frustration, defeat, and punishment. Nevertheless, in competent hands and favorable circumstances, an independent posture can survive minor infractions, provided that the Law of Power is observed meticulously.

DISSIDENCE

The dissident posture differs from independence—and from the Establishment—in its tendency to oppose and defy. The dissident's is a calculated strategy for gaining attention and support by attacking others, keeping them off balance, and amassing a string of victories. This strategy is a difficult one to carry off, because the dissident is a nuisance, distrusted and disliked all around. But the posture is not impossible. An exceptionally competent dissident can be effective in bringing about change—and establishing his position in the process.

Although willing to lock horns, the intelligent dissident

cannot afford to be haphazard in his selection of issues. Despite his belligerence, he makes it difficult for opponents to stick the label *contentious* on him, because he avoids petty disputes. He cannot be tagged meddlesome, because he steers clear of conflicts where his involvement might appear gratuitous. Moreover, his criticism is constructive: He offers positive counterproposals.

A winning dissident picks his own fights, his own field of battle, and his own timing. He makes certain that the odds are heavily in his favor. His aim is to establish a reputation as a *consistent* winner who gets things done, and who has gained a substantial following in the process. A defeat is a matter of deep concern. Dissidents make enemies. But they are more cautious than they appear to be. Not that they refuse to take chances. They know they must accept risks; but they also expend much energy minimizing the dangers to themselves.

People may challenge a dissident, carrying the fight into his territory. He is likely to duck their jabs and launch fresh attacks over issues of his own choosing. He avoids being held to a defensive position, answering charges leveled by opponents in keeping with their timetable. The dissident strategy calls for forcing others to defend themselves against a strong counterattack. To be sure, flexibility is often necessary. Nevertheless, it is a mistake for a dissident to let himself be more than moderately influenced by opponents, lest he become a mirror image of them. Originality is important to his posture.

A strategy of dissidence does not contemplate gaining notoriety for its own sake. Displays of strength are intended to gain support. Contests require careful selection and meticulous preparation. Issues should be important enough to make victory worthwhile. Yet the Laws of Power and Group Survival must not be flouted by a dissident. The counterthrusts of an aroused and united management group would be formidable.

In preparation for battle, a successful dissident must line up support, especially among the heavyweights. Allies are informed of intentions; there are no surprises among friends. It is a mistake to encourage subordinates to pick fights with others. On the contrary, it is better policy to defuse the bitterness that dissident tactics inevitably provoke. The dissident should maintain an appearance of friendly relations, even while planning the next attack.

WINNERS AND LOSERS

The four basic strategies for politicking by individuals have one motive in common: personal aggrandizement in competition. Regardless of which strategy is employed, competition will produce either conflict or compromise. When compromise is unpractical or unwanted, organizational processes ineluctably grind out a winning side and a losing side. It becomes advisable, therefore, to consider proper behavior on the part of winners and losers.

A winner may select his options in dealing with losers. He may let them be, or he may hold the door open to reconciliation. There is no need to announce victory, and certainly none to boast of it. Pursuing a loser in retreat gives her a chance to gain sympathy as an underdog. Treat her as an equal—almost, but not quite—and hope she will sink into oblivion. It is good strategy to be gracious toward the vanquished while stripping them of prerogatives.

George Roberts opts instead for full reconciliation with the losers. He is concerned about a future need for their support. Therefore, he won't insist on their suffering unnecessarily. They are allowed to recover, so long as George's position is not impaired. He may go so far as to offer a title or reward, especially one that would split the subdued leader away from the jealous among his followers. All the while, of course, George keeps a watchful eye on the losers. If they should begin to manifest peculiar tendencies—like challenging his authority—he may want to reconsider his initial decision. "Not every loser is reconcilable; some would rather go," George has concluded.

The decision to work with·a loser in the hope of winning (or buying) his support is not nearly as dangerous as it may seem. It is, in fact, often the safest and soundest course of all. By offering generous concessions and demonstrating a willingness to patch up differences, Arthur Gordon casts a heavy onus of dissent on those who would revive old disputes. In addition, by listening to ideas, accepting some suggestions, and making realistic compromises, he has occasionally gained significant advantages for himself.

Not all winners favor moderation. Specifically, the Machiavellians believe that reconciliation with a defeated adversary plays into his hands. "When you make concessions to an opponent, whether you've beaten him or not, you look weak while he gains strength," is an erroneous view. Even if there were a modicum of truth in that theory, it would still face great odds, because harsh treatment fosters reactions in kind. It encourages hostility, scheming, and retaliation.

To beat their way out of a dilemma, many executives have resorted to a device first reported by Machiavelli himself. Attaining the top position, a company president resolved to get rid of all the *enemies* he had conquered, lest they band together and overthrow him. So he brought in an executive vice president whom he encouraged to harass, badger, and bully people. This VP forced resignations, persuaded some to leave, and dismissed others. When the *deadwood* had been cleared away, news of grave offenses reached the president's ear, and he was properly horrified. On behalf of the loyal employees who remained, the president sent his VP packing. The purge was over—until a new crop of enemies arose.

Old though this script is, it remains one of the most popular ploys in organizations of all kinds. Yet the fired vice presidents go on asking, "What did I do wrong?" If such a VP is lucky, his reference may read: "Mr. Slaughter revitalized a moribund organization, thereby eliminating his own job." With or without such a reference, the VP victim is pursued by a certain animus. His next employer will probably want to abuse him in the same manner.

Which option is best? The answer will depend on several factors. The image one wants to project will lead to a tough or reasonable or forgiving stance. The strength, attitudes, and tactics of the other side may shut off one option or another. The circumstances surrrounding a victory may exert an influence. Nevertheless, it is unwise to write off the chances for reconciliation too soon. Even the most rigid opponent should be given an opportunity to come around. He just might take it.

In any case, a winner must never continue to fight beyond the truce. Any attempt to destroy the losing side or inflict additional wounds will turn the rest of the organization against you. People don't live easily with vindictiveness—not even people who had sided with the winner in the past.

If it's important to act graciously on winning, a far greater urgency attaches to proper conduct on the part of a loser. The idea is to avoid working your way into a corner permanently. Drop the fight gracefully and offer your services to the victor. Then wait for evidence of his intentions toward you, while you prepare either to join his endeavors or to defend against his maneuvers. It is not necessary to give up any authority voluntarily. Wait until the attempt is made to wrest it from you, and then see what you can salvage by negotiation. Perhaps in agreeing to give up one item at a time, you can gain concessions in return. With foresight and good bargaining, you may come out ahead after all.

Immediately after suffering a loss is no time to line up allies for the future. Your strength has eroded. It is risky for others to show signs of alliance with you, although you may receive a few clandestine expressions of sympathy. And since the urgency is gone, you can now afford to wait until someone seeks to enlist your support. You may be in a better position to offer help by then. Meanwhile, waste no time in dropping hints outside the company that you aren't altogether happy. After all, you obviously aren't riding the crest of a wave. That's reason enough to be on the lookout for better opportunities elsewhere.

11

TACTICAL PLOYS

REGARDLESS OF the basic postures people assume, the organization inevitably shapes their activities. Budgets impose control, work measurement prods the tempo, systems hold individuals accountable, and checkreins restrict their freedom. Beset by fiendish devices, the individual has little choice but to comply—on the surface. However, there are at least as many devious ways to beat systems as there are variants of the systems themselves. Beating the budget, the work-measurers, the accountability systems, and the organization chart has become a major preoccupation of people up and down the line.

BEATING THE BUDGET

The budget game is ubiquitous. It is played for high stakes under well-defined, albeit informal, rules. Furthermore, it has the elements of a major sport: risk, reward, and expertise. As with any other game, a thorough knowledge of the rules is essential to the development of winning tactics. Accordingly, a brief explanation of budgeting methods will lay the groundwork for a pragmatic approach to beating the game.

Budget jargon will be used freely in this chapter so you will be familiar with the buzz words when the budgeteers try to dazzle you with their technical nomenclature. To begin with, the discussion will follow four categories: *objectives, methods, techniques,* and *assumptions*—all standard budget terms.

The objectives of budgeting are threefold: *coordination, planning,* and *control.* Let's see what these terms mean, in practice.

Coordination of activities becomes increasingly important as a company grows. It wouldn't do to have a company's sales force bring in orders that the production department could not fill, nor to schedule production while neglecting to purchase raw materials, hire workers, and raise money to pay their wages. Because coordination is essential to the company, the Law of Group Survival makes it plain that individuals must be eager to cooperate. Translated into practice, cooperation, in this instance, means being on time with budget estimates. Individual survival demands that formulating the budget receive priority treatment. Expert, influential planners will accept nothing less of the organization, even while the Law of Self-Interest leads them to proclaim that they don't want the budget process to get in the way of regular activities. (*Their* survival is at stake, too.)

While cooperation with the budget process involves timeliness, it does not demand accuracy. Indeed, everyone is well aware of the limits imposed by human fallibility. Few people claim to be seers, but anyone who sets his mind to it can turn out plausible estimates. Plausible, not accurate. For reasons which will become clear, it is essential to incorporate supporting data suitably *fudged* to bring out plausible (and, it need hardly be added, self-serving) results.

Planning for an activity involves estimating the staff that will be needed and the expenditures that will be incurred. This is the stage where experts employ a variety of techniques to manipulate data and beat the budget.

When Arthur Gordon became marketing vice president, he wanted a large allocation of funds for advertising. Since his company's advertising budget was based on projected sales, Arthur inclined toward optimism in forecasting the volumes that would be attained. By the time he was called to account for a shortfall in actual sales, Arthur had long since committed all budgeted funds. That, of course, was his real aim. Just think how much lower sales might have fallen without Arthur's inflated advertising expenditures! The next year, Arthur's forecast was greeted with skepticism, which he overcame with elaborate charts. In later years, he had to compromise, but only after protracted negotiation during which he repeatedly pointed to the year in which sales actually exceeded expectations. (That happens, sometimes, even to sanguine forecasters. And when an extraordinarily good year is in the offing, low-balling the forecast can be good strategy.)

A manager in George Roberts's department has built an empire over the years, and she is reluctant to lose it. Yet she must face the annual assaults of the budgeteers who persistently chip away a little here and a little there. "You got along on so much last year. Next year we expect you to do better. A ten percent cut is reasonable enough. That's what we're asking everyone else to accept." The first time Maggie heard that song, she had enough *slack* in her budget to be able to stand a cut easily. In fact, she could well afford several annual cuts; so she came to be known for her splendid attitude. She still has a reputation as a manager who cooperates in promoting budgetary efficiency, but the game has changed. Maggie manages to stay ahead now by introducing slack in the new elements of her budget every year. She picks out items that were not in the previous year's budget. To these items, she adds a few that, she argues, have changed significantly. Since all these items are now on a new footing, unrelated to the past, Maggie is able to lard them with sufficient slack to ensure comfortable operating conditions in her department. She can afford to laugh quietly at the budget-tightening game; she is beating it.

George, having learned a bitter lesson at a previous company, is happy to cooperate with Maggie now. In those days, George played the budget game straight, poor innocent, tightening up on his own initiative and running an unusually efficient department. When the ukase came to cut staff, he was at his wit's end trying to find a way to cope with an impossible situation. Not only was there no fat to trim, but George was afraid that the survivors of an unfair cutback would never again feel the same sense of loyalty to him or his company. In fact, George was properly concerned that his people might never again be as productive as they had been. Other managers, perceiving the predicament George was in, were delighted to watch this competitive threat being run through the wringer. They professed to see no reason why George couldn't accept the same sacrifices that everyone else was being called on to make. In the end, George's island of superefficiency would go down the drain, a victim of budget politics. George himself moved to another company. No one can afford to do too good a job in the modern organization. The risk is awesome.

Susan Williams liked conducting pilot projects on her own, but she found that the process of getting funds was just too much trouble. So she juggled her budget, inflating items wherever she could, in order to cover the expenditures she wanted to make. Year-to-year comparisons of Susan's budget requests were reasonable; so everyone was satisfied, especially Susan.

All budgeting is political, but some types of budgets are more susceptible to politicking than others. The examples above dealt mainly with budgets that controlled operations. *Operating budgets*, as they are called, are generally the least political of all. However, at one point—allocations for Arthur's advertising contracts—the discussion turned to expenditures that are subject to management decision. These *discretionary budgets*, which management is free to vary within broad limits, automatically become intensely political. Another intensely political set of items are *transfer prices*, which companies within the affiliated group are permitted to charge each other for intracorporate sales. Since these transfer prices affect earnings on both sides of all intracorporate transactions, bargaining can become quite hard, and final settlements are political compromises.

Besides operating and discretionary budgets, there are *capital budgets*, which are completely political. The funds that will be allocated to one major project and denied to another are determined on the basis of political clout. When limited funds are available for allocation, and proposals include building a new plant in Des Moines, extending an old plant in Baltimore, or establishing general warehouses at strategic locations around the country, *feasibility studies* may be ordered to evaluate the economic practicality of competing plans. But when all the calculations have been made—return on investment (ROI), discounted cash flow (DCF), risk analysis, decision analysis, and sensitivity analysis—bargaining begins in earnest. In the end, decisions must be political, which is to say that the results of the process, taken as a whole, must be such that the most powerful group is willing and able to impose them and the less powerful groups are ready to accept them.

Control is the phase of budgeting in which *feedback*, in the form of operating reports, is compared with budget figures. The differences, or *variances*, which may be either *favorable* or *unfavorable*, are analyzed until some people are needled and others are hanged. Obviously, managers who succeed in getting *loose* budgets approved in an early stage are less likely to be troubled by unfavorable variances, or budget *overruns*, later. It's the managers with *tight* budgets who have to anticipate problems. But a moment's reflection on what has already been said about budget tightening in successive years will lead to the conclusion that true budget artistry is concerned not with budget overruns, but with eliminating, or rather forestalling, *favorable variances*. That's right. A favorable variance will be attacked by the budgeteers as evidence of slack; next year they will want to tighten up. Consequently, for survival in the budget game, it becomes important to anticipate favorable variances and to take *remedial action* (a favorite budgeteering phrase, but not in the same sense that is intended here) without delay. Get those allocated funds spent before time runs out, hire that replacement whether another person is needed or not—and do it fast! In government agencies, where allocations may expire at the end of the fiscal year, it becomes doubly important to spend every *appropriated* dollar on time, lest the current year's allotment and next year's battle of the budget are lost together.

Budgeting methods and techniques need not be discussed in detail here, beyond what has already been mentioned in passing. It is worth noting, however, that only *flexible* budgets are capable of automatically adjusting standards to actual volume levels. A flexible budget is really a series of budgets based on identical assumptions, except that volumes vary. Accordingly, in a company with ordinary (nonflexible) budgets—without adjustments for variations in volume—it is worthwhile for managers to attribute their variances to *volume differentials* whenever possible, thus: "We can't cut our staff, because we don't want to lose trained people with temporary layoffs. So when the sales department falls below its quota, our department must suffer the impact of low volume on our unit cost." That is the basic defense until flexible budgeting comes along. Meanwhile, few bosses will be prepared to counter the *volume variance* argument.

Another strong defense for managers faced with unfavorable variances raises the issue of *controllability*. When local property taxes rise, or a new method of depreciation raises the charges to operations, managers are entitled to complain of unfair treatment. Likewise, if power costs are *allocated* to departments arbitrarily, an increase in one's share should be contested. In a word, *one should not be held responsible for expenses he can do nothing about.* The budgeteers will agree, for they are fair-minded, if cold-hearted, people.

Budget assumptions offer a manager additional room for maneuvering, provided that top management spells out, in writing, the assumptions the budget is based on. In working on her own budget, a manager should seize every opportunity these assumptions afford; later, she should try to pin every variance on erroneous assumptions made by others. Here's how it works.

Susan's expenditures for supplies ran over budget, and she was asked, "How come?" Discovering that prices for some items were up as much as 25 percent, whereas the purchasing department had predicted a rise of only 10 percent overall, Susan was in the clear. When sales fell short of Arthur's estimate, he pointed out that earlier predictions of gross national product and of his industry's output, as projected with the aid of an *input/output chart* and promulgated by top management, were higher than actually achieved. It was not Arthur's place to second-guess top management, so he was home free. In rationalizing variances, managers too often neglect basic budget assumptions made by others. These superb defensive shields deserve more attention.

To summarize, a beleaguered manager has several escape hatches whenever he is called on to explain his department's variances from budget. The budget assumptions announced by others can provide helpful exculpatory arguments. Allocated expenses or other noncontrollable items make excellent excuses. And volume variance can be used in special circumstances. However, it is still better to work slack into a budget beforehand, and to obviate favorable variances whenever they threaten to create an unstable situation.

Program budgeting has introduced new hazards for some managers, especially in government. Wherever program budgeting (also called PPBS, for planning-programming-budgeting system) overrides the old *line-item* budget (which stops at detailing departmental expenses by category), it becomes necessary to justify requests for funding on the basis of overall results to be achieved by a total program, instead of merely relying on simple departmental comparisons with past expenditures of similar nature. When results (output) become the measure of a program's social value, to be compared with expenditures (input) in a *cost/effectiveness* analysis, bureaucrats must face a different sort of challenge. They must begin to justify their activities in terms of *fulfilling the purposes of enabling legislation*, and not merely in terms of essentially meaningless ratios like spending per employee, per office, or per month. Although program budgeting is quite logical, many managers in government prefer to oppose the concept on the specious grounds that it is complex or unwieldy; other people vainly attempt to associate PPBS with doubtful programs. In the end, sophistication is likely to prevail. Program budgeting and its control counterpart, *performance auditing*, cannot be beaten down forever. They will resurface under one name or another. So, those managers who are in government, be forewarned. Rationalization will become increasingly difficult under program budgeting.

WORK-MEASUREMENT

Spectators at a track meet learn to recognize outstanding performers by the ease with which they glide around the track, leaving in their wake the hard-working turf-pounders. Yet no one has ever thought to stand athletic competition on its head by rewarding exertion instead of achievement. The race is to the swift.

By contrast, recognition of accomplishment has given way to more exciting games in business. Results count, of course —everyone says so—but they are relatively easy to measure with but little ingenuity. So there has been a great rush to measure input instead. The lore of industrial engineering has so imbued management thought with the concept of measuring input instead of output, that it no longer pays —if it ever did—for anyone to take things in stride and make his job look easy. Whereas the star athlete is the one who accomplishes his mission with consummate grace, the star executive is the one who keeps busy, spending the correct numbers of hours in conferring, reporting, inspecting, directing, and so on. Not that anyone has ever pronounced what the correct numbers should be. Statistical studies merely summarize the guesses of randomly selected samples. The leap from reported averages to normative guides is studiously avoided by authors. But not by their readers—and there's the rub. Accordingly, one secret of survival is to follow customary time-allocations. An outgrowth of this method is an inability to find time for essential matters; and this insufficiency of time serves to make the job look more difficult— the Law of Fugling, pragmatically applied.

Executives are entreated to measure and control their own allocation of time to various activities. "But time is easy to measure, and the value of an idea is not; so the industrial engineers are avoiding difficulty after all": That may sound like a valid objection, but it isn't. First, ideas are only intermediate output. In business, final results are indeed relatively easy to measure. Second, if subconscious thinking is included, as it should be, then those who purport to measure time are only wasting it. No, industrial engineers are not lazy; they are not looking for easy ways out. On the contrary, they eschew the obvious for the esoteric. When they see a clerk performing a repetitive task, they will measure the percentage of his time that is lost in walking, talking, idleness, and attention to personal needs. Then, with *pace-rating* techniques, they will diligently determine how fast the clerk is working, in order to evaluate the clerk's use of his productive time. Surely a less educated person might stumble on a more direct method for measuring performance: by counting the output. (To give credit where it is due, scheduling assignments of short duration is an engineer's method that does effectively measure and control output.)

A favorite work-measurement method of industrial engineers is a contribution of the statisticians, called *work-sampling* or *ratio delay*. Briefly, readings of activities are taken at random intervals, in order to ascertain how people are spending their time: for example, 20 percent in reading; 10 percent in writing; 8 percent in sorting and assembling papers; 15 percent in telephone conversations; 12 percent away from desk, etc. (It must be acknowledged that a work-sampling study can produce dramatic results when used for certain purposes. For example, before purchasing office machines for a group of employees, it is useful to know what portion of the group's time is spent in chores that would be helped by specific machines.)

Knowingly or unknowingly, many managers have adapted work-sampling to informal use, for estimating crudely how subordinates split their working hours between productive labors and nonproductive *lost time*. Assuredly, such informal readings provide some idea of the impression whole departments are making on visitors from the higher echelons. Incidentally, supervisors ought to encourage networks to signal the approach of a VIP. It is to a supervisor's advantage to alert his people to perk up at those times. And for supervisors themselves, the best time to fugle is when a visiting bigwig is in the area.

To return to the methodology of the informal work-sample: Immediately on stepping out of his office, George Roberts takes note of what each person in a group is doing.

Fairly frequent observations of this nature are easily made. Since these informal observations are not truly random—they would have to be timed in advance with the aid of a table of random numbers for that—firm conclusions are unwarranted. To illustrate the dangers of nonrandom observations, George may unwittingly be following a recurrent pattern that coincides with a pattern among his staff. He may leave his office to head for daily meetings with his boss at the same time that his people take a coffee break, or he may regularly come out to look for a certain flash report just when several people simultaneously and legitimately take a few minutes for themselves. When randomness is a requisite, regularity is not a virtue. Sometimes however, a sizable number of scattered observations may permit tentative inferences concerning a group's ratio of work to nonwork activities.

For those subordinates who want to beat George's adaptation of work-sampling, the busy-bee technique is a defense against all observation methods, formal and informal, that purport to measure input. People who find their work taken away by a computer often create other chores to keep themselves busy. They shuffle papers, gathering, sorting, re-sorting, arranging, and sometimes distributing them. All needless effort, but who would guess that from their apparent determination to get things done? Some respite themselves by striding through the corridors at a rapid pace, clutching sheets of paper in their hands and looking for all the world like people on an urgent mission. Walking too slowly arouses suspicion; carrying too many papers at one time looks like a messenger's work; but experts at the busy-bee technique make detection difficult.

At higher levels, the act looks different, but its purpose is substantially the same. The managers who put in long hours, and then take papers home, appear to be pictures of industriousness, dedicated servants of the company. Their cluttered desks, overflowing to tables and window sills, are meant to convey an image of the overburdened executive. In fact, they may be spending their time staring emptily at the pages before them or wasting their efforts on meaningless generalities and repetitious detail. They may memorize some data for a few days and seize an opportunity to show off an amazing grasp of figures. They are frequently heard to complain that they can never grapple with the larger problems facing the company, because they are perpetually bogged down in details that others ought to handle, except that no one can be trusted to do things well enough.

Since executives of this type—and there are plenty of them —are incapable of training a staff, and their expressed evaluations of their people are derogatory, it is little wonder that the people under them get nowhere. Not only do subordinates find their progress blocked within the company, but their potential value to other companies suffers as well. So they find it hard to move. In a word, they are trapped. Survival requires assessing these situations quickly and getting out.

To sum up, the way to survive the work-measurement philosophy depends on one's position. For instance, a manager who has everything running smoothly had better not sit back to enjoy life while congratulating himself on his organizing talent as an administrator. He is better advised to look busy—harassed, if possible—even if he has to create work for himself. (Running a business of one's own on the side is dangerous, and it creates a bad impression among one's customers; but it can be done.) The work-ethic demeanor is a valid application of the Law of Fugling. So much so that the same manager can make limited use of informal work-sampling to tell him whether his staff is following his example by looking busy enough to keep the top executives happy.

At lower levels, too, the idea is to look busy, for the sake of yourself, your group, and your boss. Appearance is everything, so long as input (effort) is being measured instead of output (production). A problem arises when one uncovers an incompetent boss who is successfully posturing as a hard-working mainstay of the company. If he is truly inept, the situation is bad, and the prognosis is worse. It will probably be necessary to arrange a transfer or find another job—the sooner the better.

THE ACCOUNTABILITY SYSTEMS

Sophisticated accounting systems produce *departmental operating reports,* whose purpose is to hold managers responsible for the financial results of their departments and for variances from their *departmental budgets.* Procedures call for signatures or initials on all documents, including schedules and notes, at the same time that memo pads carry slogans urging people to "put it in writing—nothing by mouth." Although the purpose of these control mechanisms is always to hold individuals responsible for whatever may go wrong, there is nothing to stop a person from utilizing a control procedure when he wants to go on record, claim credit, or prove his frugality. None of this is considered devious, so far. But for the adventurous, there are sly ways to take advantage of accountability systems, and for the wary, there are tortuous ploys to guard against.

Initialing one's own documents is an act of compliance with the rules. Although it is time-consuming for a manager to initial all documents emanating from his department, the presence of his initials testifies to his awareness of departmental activities. The practice is therefore commendable. True artistry begins with creating opportunities for signing a wide assortment of documents, and particularly those that convey fresh ideas. This tactic is manifestly of greatest use in companies operating at multiple locations. People at a distance often experience some difficulty in distinguishing between legitimate signatures and superfluous ones.

Susan Williams found certain executives frequently expressing interest in her work. Invariably, they would ask to see her reports before release. Susan learned why. Before long, these people were asking for acknowledgment of their contributions, "only, of course, if you agree"; but it's difficult to turn down that simple request coming from the executive levels.

Susan learned a trick or two herself. When a memorandum came her way, she drafted marginal comments for circulation to her own list of favored people. Any project that fell within Susan's specialty was likely to feature her signature prominently. She signed letters of transmittal, unless someone up the line took over. She also discovered that computer printouts were like orphans ready for adoption by anyone willing to put a covering letter on excerpts. She was willing.

Susan rightly distrusts offers that permit her to sign reports or releases. She instinctively suspects duplicity. There must be a trap somewhere! Perhaps the report is a trial balloon, or it will offend vested interests, or it subtly challenges someone's position. After all, it is worth some form of recompense to be a signatory. Why would anyone give away something of value, without even suggesting a quid pro quo?

Accounting controls can be circumvented by a different bag of tricks. George Roberts made it a practice never to accept a charge if he could get someone else to take it. Rather than buy books or subscriptions for his department, he requisitioned them from the company library. Before visiting a plant, he asked the plant manager to assign an account code chargeable to that plant's administrative expense accounts. For many of his needs, George relied on the services of typing pool, print shop, and systems department, while his own budget remained lean and trim.

In many companies, a system of crosscharging would forestall George's freeloading ways. The systems department, for example, would initiate a charge to him for designing forms, writing procedures, and so on. Operating within such a system, Arthur Gordon would have found George's tactics misguided. By making use of specialists from other departments, Arthur tacitly proclaimed his enlightenment through the accounting reports which charged him for special services. These services had been made available by top management, and cooperative executives used them. Arthur sensed an opportunity for self-aggrandizement in a situation where he was the major *customer* of a service activity. Why shouldn't the organization chart eventually be redesigned so that the service department reported directly to Arthur?

THE ORGANIZATION CHART

An ambitious manager named Hal, two levels below Arthur Gordon, incautiously aroused suspicion by his conduct one day. While the department head between them was away on a short trip, Arthur and Hal met, and Arthur was astounded by a string of slurring remarks about the absent executive. Alert to the dangers of encouraging disloyalty, Arthur cut the meeting short, suggesting that it would be well to wait until alternative proposals could be reviewed and commented on by Hal's capable boss (and Arthur's trustworthy subordinate.)

On the department head's return, Arthur met with him and surveyed his defenses, which were voluminous. For here was a person who kept records of everything—notes of conversations and minutes of meetings were all there to satisfy Arthur's curiosity and convince him that ridding the department of Hal was in the best interests of the company. A dirty player lost through a combination of his own rashness, his boss's superb defense, and Arthur's playing by the rules. But on previous occasions, Hal had fared better while using the same duplicitous stratagems against other bosses.

Such activities cannot go unnoticed. A reputation for de

ceit trailed after Hal, even though he waited a long time
before showing his hand again. Then Arthur called the game
to an abrupt end. Hal's next round would have to be played
somewhere else. "You win one; you lose one." Hal won't
change.

The individual in pursuit of the Law of Aggrandizement
must observe certain niceties of organization life. Flouting
the organization chart is a dangerous stunt, inconsistent with
graceful fugling, and therefore to be avoided in general. The
defense against such misconduct involves nothing more than
normal politicking procedures: a general alertness; membership in a network; frequent, friendly contact with one's boss;
and records of significant happenings.

12

A TIME TO DECIDE

THE WORD *interdisciplinary* is fashionable now, and among the modish topics benefiting from both wide publicity and an interdisciplinary approach, *decision theory* ranks high. This book will explore neither the mathematical profundities nor the elaborate charts (*trees*) that belong to the standard apparatus of those who teach others how to be decision-makers. There has been no study to test whether the quality of business decisions is improving as a result of the use and misuse of sophisticated techniques. There is only a consensus that executive decisions on the whole are pretty bad.

Decisiveness is not characteristic of most managers. Decision-making is further hampered by the deep-seated belief of many managers in *Don't stick your neck out*. Nevertheless, decisions have to be made, and problems have to be solved. Accordingly, elaborate protocol has evolved for coping with decision processes—but not necessarily for improving them. An exploration of problem-solving and decision-making is obviously essential to those who enter organizational life with heroic ambitions.

PROBLEM-SOLVING AND
DECISION-MAKING

In order to comprehend the import of *political* decision-making, it will be useful to survey conventional theories of problem-solving, just as a good military officer surveys the terrain and troop-deployment before going into battle. The following steps are typical of standard problem-solving techniques:

• *Fact-Gathering:* the accumulation of large quantities of information (some of it relevant) from interviews, questionnaires, observations, tests, reports, and records. It is particularly important to collect the ideas of those who appear to know what goes on, in order to adopt their solutions or refute them. Although some management consultants profess to believe that a good study must go into fine detail—the more detail of all kinds, the better—others are horrified by the prospect of an inundation of trivia. A reasonable effort at data-gathering will generally suffice.

• *Analysis:* the reworking of data into patterns that conform to established dogma and preconceived notions. While some consultants trust mathematically provable methods only, others prefer to rely on intuition; straddlers like to talk about *heuristic* (nonprovable) methods in combination with mathematical approaches. For many consultants, the objective of early analysis is merely to define the problem; later analysis evaluates proposed solutions.

• *Search for Solutions:* the collecting of proposed answers to problems. A method that gained notoriety at one time, and still has its advocates, is *brainstorming,* an informal meeting in which uninhibited talk is encouraged, and participants may feel free to steal ideas from each other without acknowledging the source.

• *Decision:* the selection of a preferred solution, which will then be justified by a string of plausible rationalizations, including *cost/benefit analysis* (the relation between the sacrifices required and the objective to be attained).

Not all approaches to problem-solving fit this outline precisely. The decision tree makes it hard to tell where analysis of the problem leaves off and finding a solution begins. In this method, a series of decision points (*nodes*) resolves the overall problem into a number of smaller ones, each with perhaps two or three options (branches). If there aren't too many nodes and bifurcations—in other words, if the problem is not overly complex to begin with—then all the ramifications can be followed to their ends, and an *optimum* solution is generated.

A complication can be introduced to problem-solving by noting that *uncertainty* surrounds the results anticipated from each option. Thus *deterministic* answers give way to *probabilistic* results and *stochastic* functions (recognizing uncertainty through time), involving *risk*—an inescapable four-letter word. Now probabilities must be assigned over ranges of results, so that the risk of shortfall or failure can be assessed.

Finally, the likely effects of bad guessing are quantified with respect to individual variables. Thus, since forecasts may fall wide of the mark, *sensitivity analysis* undertakes to add yet another set of guesses to calculate how serious the first bad guesses could prove to be.

Brief though it may be—and admittedly one-sided—this description of conventional problem-solving stages is adaptable to political decision-making. The adaptation that follows is in conformity with the Laws of Aggrandizement, Constraints, Influence, and Power, because pragmatic decisions must conform to the laws of the organization if the decision-maker is to survive.

SOPHISTICATED DECISION-MAKING

Decisions are made by those who are not deterred by organizational oppressiveness, sniping by competitors, or feelings of insecurity. If a person wants to have something to say about how things are done, how can he minimize personal risk while exerting an influence on decisions? One answer is to play lacrosse. A common situation in lacrosse pits two opposing players against each other in pursuit of a ball that is exquisitely neutral. One player goes after the ball, attempting to retrieve it with his stick, while the second player goes after the first player, applying a body check. In this conflict of tactics, the second player wins. He removes his opponent from the play and goes on to recover the ball. "Play the man, not the ball," is the coach's advice.

Decision theory must be interpreted in the light of this injunction to play the man instead of the ball. To illustrate, Arthur Gordon was appointed to a capital-budget committee that was to select projects for funding by the company. How should these planners evaluate the relative merits of alternative proposals? The answer: by adhering rigidly to the following steps:

Fact-Finding. Unquestionably, it is important to have facts at one's fingertips when entering the decision process. But which facts are truly pertinent? In practice, the most important facts are the ones most often overlooked. Here is a list of essential information for the guidance of the sophisticated decision-maker:

1. What does my boss think? Is he favorably disposed toward each option, unfavorably disposed, or indifferent?

2. Have others expressed their opinions? Where do they stand? Can they be persuaded to shift their positions? How (politically) strong are the people lined up for and against each option?

3. Who may be hurt by each option? How strong are

these persons or groups? Can any of them be disarmed, neutralized, mollified, or indemnified?

4. Who stands to gain from each option? Will one person's gain be interpreted ipso facto as another's relative loss of status? If so, what can be done about that? Can some of the gain be diverted to myself?

5. Who will oppose my acting on this matter, and how strong are they? Should I end-play them, ignore them, or prepare to counteract their anticipated response?

Analysis. When facts have been gathered, the analytical stage proceeds to develop a logical conclusion. Salient points in an analysis of each option include:

1. What alliances can be expected to develop against me? What are the probabilities that various combinations will form? How strong will these alliances be? What are the mathematical values (strengths multiplied by probabilities) of the various combinations?

2. What natural allies do I have? How reliable are they? What is the strength of each? What is the aggregate mathematical value of my prospective allies, considering their strengths and reliabilities?

3. Which potential allies should I cultivate? What is my probability of success in cultivating each? What is the strength of each? Hence, what is the mathematical value (probability of success multiplied by strength) of each potential ally? What would I have to do to win each one over? What concessions will I be called on to make?

4. In summarizing all the mathematical values, how should I realistically evaluate my chances of success? As to methodology, when people begin to respond, what go/no-go points should I establish for myself?

Risk and Sensitivity. The foregoing analysis includes calculations of the probabilities of success or failure in winning people over to each option, as well as the payoffs and probabilities of realizing each level of payoff. In addition, it is well to calculate the risks adhering to each option and potential effects of certain possible miscalculations. To assess these factors properly, decision-makers must weigh such variables as these:

1. The separate consequences of (a) suffering a loss in seeing my actions rejected, rebuffed, attacked, or criticized by others; and (b) having to abandon my program as a failure after setting it in motion.

2. The probabilities that resistance will in fact hamper the implementation of my program. Also the countermeasures that will be available, their political cost, and their probabilities of success.

3. Aggregate losses that may be sustained, in consideration of the consequences enumerated above and their probabilities. This is the total risk.

4. Expected effects of underestimating the strength of the opponents or miscalculating the strength of the allies, or errors in other estimates. What would be salvageable in retreat? These considerations are related to individual political sensitivity analysis.

By way of recapitulation, *note that the significant information has virtually nothing to do with the options themselves, but only with the people who are affected by them.* That is what truly sophisticated decision-making means. The concept goes a long way toward explaining why so many decisions are bad, from the standpoint of the company as a whole. If this conclusion conflicts with the Law of Group Survival, remember that the effects of a poor decision are not known until later (often long afterward), when it is difficult to cut through the deft misrepresentation and spreading of blame.

THE POLITICS OF DELAY

The complexity of the decision process explains why inaction and delay are often preferred to active decision-making.

Despite serious efforts at garnering data about individual impacts and views, an analysis may be incomplete. Sometimes Arthur's confrères conclude that they are in no position to judge the value and risk to themselves in choosing one option or another. At other times, they recognize a no-win situation. Delays are common (and useful) enough to warrant an investigation of their rationale and techniques.

In party politics, the timing of some decisions is of tremendous importance. In selecting issues for a campaign, the early birds may end up eating worms, and they run risks of finding themselves out of touch with the voters as sentiment shifts later on. So the professional politicians hold back, hoping not only to acquire better information, but also to watch their bargaining power increase as their party comes closer to the moment of truth. However, the waiting game runs risks of its own: Once others arrive at agreements, late joiners may be regarded with aloofness. In addition, prolonged delay suggests indecisiveness, which has its drawbacks among one's followers.

The advantages and disadvantages of the waiting game apply in company politics, too. Delays must be carried off gracefully; they must maintain an appearance of judicious conduct; and they should be supported by a rationale. For instance, no matter how much information is available, it is proper to call for a survey that will gather more; in turn, time allocations should be sufficiently large to permit a detailed analysis of facts, so that proper conclusions may be reached; additional time should be allowed for preparing a persuasive presentation.

Committees are frequently appointed as instruments of delay. Large numbers are best for the purpose, because they experience more difficulty in agreeing on anything. In addition, since each member must be allotted time to speak, larger groups can be counted on for longer meetings and shorter agendas that accomplish less. Selection of an Ad Hoc Committee for Delaying Project Alpha requires care; a single contentious member can often hobble progress well enough, but several members at odds with each other offer a more efficacious impediment to the proceedings. Unquestionably, discussions with appointed members can be used to convey a desire for stalling. Once that message is understood, dilatory tactics will dominate.

While committees can be useful in delaying action, they are not essential to the imaginative strategist. Another effective technique calls for giving individual assignments and designating them *low-priority* items. It shouldn't take an intelligent novice too long to figure out that such items form a permanent work backlog that contributes to his peace of mind. If he were to tackle his low-priority list too soon, it might make the company wonder if his work load was too light and his job dispensable. Among the low-priority items, there should be assignments of rather large dimensions, just to be sure they can't all be completed, even by some unenlightened plodder whose eagerness outstrips his comprehension of practicalities. Meanwhile, the delayer himself is always prepared to respond to queries. This item or that is "on the back burner; it comes up occasionally, but no one has found the time to do the spadework for a proper study."

When delay is in order, it is always feasible to assemble recruits for the delaying project, just as one would enlist people for any other purpose. Initial soundings will disclose the people who have a natural bent in the right direction. They are undoubtedly known already, among their colleagues, as the people who offer such comments as these: "The last time we tried that, it took months to straighten things out again," or "That's one of those things that somebody new is always coming up with. You can't blame them really, because it sounds good; but we've wasted more time than I care to remember proving over and over that it won't work." Assigning a study project to such a person is a safe way to stall it, and very likely to kill it outright. As an added benefit, careful delegation of this sort, giving a negatively oriented person a chance to exercise the Law of Influence, might improve your interpersonal relations.

Some of the foregoing observations lead to a question that must be answered: Why delay a decision? Why not decide at once against action, thereby removing an issue from the list of open items?

Valid reasons often militate against decisive negative action. It may be wise to avoid offending the sponsor of a proposal. Let someone else do that. In other circumstances, delay may be advisable in order to wait for a more favorable climate of opinion. Indeed, additional time may be needed to take soundings before determining whether to take a stand at all.

For killing a proposal, there are methods ranging from a crude No, to applications of the Law of Self-Interest, to the devious antics of Susan Williams's former boss. Bring him a proposal of any kind and he becomes wildly enthusiastic about it—at first. Then he sets about building up something huge—and eventually monstrous. Start with a proposal to provide hospitalization coverage for the staff, and before long he will ask for a full program of fringe benefits encompassing major medical, group life, pensions, and deferred profit-sharing all at once, plus a subsidized cafeteria, company cars, low-interest loans to executives, stock options, and gift packages to employees. In the end, after expenditure of substantial effort in whipping up all sorts of proposals and discussing a great many matters with a number of outside advisors, the time comes for decision. Now Susan's boss, feigning shock and disappointment, finds the package much too costly. It's too late to bring him back to the original suggestion. The issue is dead. Moreover, even if Susan had spurned the ploy at an early stage, a neophyte would have been found to collaborate in a supporting role.

Susan also watched her boss's technique for handling salespersons importuning for favorable decisions. He simply gave them all the time they asked, closing each session with

an expression of willingness to listen and explore further—
but without a commitment. In the end, even the most persistent of salespersons called off his meetings with Susan's
boss. The meetings took too much of his time, for here
was a man apparently willing to go on forever. The technique worked well against overly aggressive fund-raisers, too.
Whereas negative responses may lead a fund-raiser to recite
his carefully rehearsed counterarguments and increase the
pressure, genial time-wasting will eventually persuade him
to cut the conversation short. For people who can afford the
time loss themselves, the method works.

THE ORDEAL OF DECIDING

It is possible to put off issuing a categorical statement while
indicating a mild preference that can be withdrawn without
embarrassment, if necessary, and that invites comments from
others. Taking a partial stand seems reasonable enough.
However, a simple memorandum saying, in effect, "This proposal doesn't bother me. How do you people feel about it?"
will be received by different people in different ways, depending on their level relative to the sender.

If a manager sends such a question to the supervisors
under him, they will perceive that the scales are tipped in
favor of the proposal. They are likely to go along. Even the
show-offs who usually vie with each other to predict difficulties will be inclined to minimize the problems they
foresee.

However, if the addressees are at the same managerial
level as the sender, he will be suspected of stealing a march,
intruding on the territories of others, usurping their authority, and so on. "I was just about to offer a proposal of my
own," will be heard from several quarters. "After having
studied the matter for several months, I can tell you that
there are considerably more ramifications to the problem

than I had originally expected to find. If you had taken the trouble to make a similar study, your findings would not have permitted you to offer these suggestions seriously." Someone will say, "Your proposal is full of holes. There are at least a dozen situations I can think of immediately that are not covered. For instance, what would happen if . . . ?" A series of similar attacks can destroy a proposal; and it will probably be revived later by someone else, who will then take credit for being able to get things done—and rightly so, because he will have prepared the groundwork for a successful drive.

To avoid the inherent problems of dealing with peers, requests for decisions may be sent up the chain of command. Now the same words—How do you feel about this?—take on a new significance; the nature of the request is somehow different. The decision process is out of the hands of the person who sends a proposal upstairs. She may be asked for details and questioned about possible effects; her opinion may be sought; but the decision will be handed down to her.

Before taking a stand, it is often advantageous to induce prospective opponents to fire the first round. Perhaps one can afford to sit back and wait for the attack to come, but there are occasions when it is better to draw fire early. How does Arthur Gordon accomplish that, without giving away his own position? He has several methods.

A trial balloon invites attack. Better still, by wording a statement so carefully as to avoid taking sides, Arthur may be lucky enough to force opponents out into the open first. Then, with full knowledge of their position, he can avert certain difficulties. The method is to raise an issue, present both sides while maintaining a neutral posture, and invite expressions of opinion. Those who fail to respond now can be criticized when they object later.

In lieu of sending up a trial balloon, Arthur may elect to conduct a full-scale survey. By asking others' opinions and garnering information, he may be able to preclude an incipient opposition from further development.

Whenever a proposal affects two or more activities, the decision to accept must come from an authority that controls both activities. Since interaction between activities is extensive in all organizations, bigness itself tends to discourage decision-making at lower levels. There are just too many people to contend with. However, the Law of Influence can be made to work for individuals who want to use it for personal survival.

Since sprawling companies discourage decision-making without altogether precluding it, there is room for individual styles and differing behavior-patterns. Despite discouragement, a great many minor decisions are made at the middle levels by a hard core of self-confident, courageous people without whom no company could operate for long. These are the unsung heroes, the competent minority who pull most of the load. They are both capable and foolish. By taking things into their own hands, they keep the company going; but by doing their work quietly, they relinquish the credit for routine success to others—who eagerly seize it— while accepting exposure to blame for whatever goes wrong.

The logic of the situation leads to divergent approaches. On the one hand, those whose well-developed instinct for gambling urges them to accept large risks in hopes of commensurate rewards, almost seem to go out of their way to look for trouble. But, for all that, they know what they're up to. When others are marching in unison, you can attract attention by being out of step. (The superficial analogy to dissidence is obvious, but aggressive decision-makers are not true dissidents.)

Arthur Gordon gave that tactic a fling for a while, making decisions that increased his exposure to attack. To further his cause, however, he simultaneously adopted a flamboyant operating style, announcing each decision with a flourish that amounted to defiance of timorous colleagues. Even when something went wrong, Arthur was ready to taunt his accusers with the contrast between his record of bold successes and their failure to act. Although envied and resented for his showmanship, Arthur was grudgingly conceded to be an effective leader.

On the other hand, the large-company climate often encourages a timorous approach. At one time, even when an issue affected no one outside his own staff, George Roberts would bring the matter to his boss for a decision. Before so much as expressing an opinion, George wanted to know what others had said. He made few mistakes on that job; but little of the company's progress could be attributed to him, even charitably.

In fairness to George, it must be admitted that the pattern of his behavior at that time was set by his company's leadership style. Adaptation to centralized leadership ineluctably led to a constriction of assumed responsibility. Earlier in his career, George had run an efficient operation. He had avoided being bogged down by a system designed primarily to control people—and not necessarily to get things done. Then, with a change in management, George acquired a new boss whose style called for looking over subordinates' shoulders, second-guessing them, and reversing their minor decisions. In time, George was conditioned to relinquishing his prerogatives, as he increasingly relied on a superior intellect to lead him. Instead of studying matters carefully himself, George fell into the habit of passing questions along. (They were going to be reviewed and revised, anyhow; so why bother to think about answers, when you don't have the last word?) Perceiving that he had no real responsibility, he lacked the will to decide issues for himself. For a while, George was thoroughly attuned to centralized management. Fortunately, a job change revitalized George's positive attitudes before too much damage had been done to him.

A little-appreciated method for ducking a decision is to pretend to be making one. When Arthur Gordon's committee *decided* to appoint a subcommittee to investigate proposals further and submit a new set of recommendations, it had clearly put off a decision. There is nothing new in misusing words to create an illusion.

A slightly—but only slightly—more subtle approach is practiced by some people under pressure to give advice they are unprepared, and often unqualified, to give. Never blinking an eye, they come up with a halfway compromise that must be announced grandly to forestall laughter. "Should I raise prices ten cents to cover increased costs?" asks a small company's president. "If I do, I'll be risking a substantial loss in sales."

"How much of your volume do you expect to lose?"

"I don't know exactly; and I'm not going to pay for a market survey."

"What figures do you have?"

"You've already seen them. They don't answer my question."

"I suggest you raise your price five cents. You might even do it on a trial basis."

Why five cents? For no better reason than that it's half of ten cents. Incredible as this conversation may appear, Susan Williams heard variations of it often at her small company. The typical large company, with its many specialists and its insistence on substantive support for conclusions, does not often tolerate such crudity. Nevertheless, large-company compromises are arrived at by negotiating methods that are frequently neither more intelligible nor more defensible. A survival strategy should include alertness to unsupportable nostrums, no matter how artfully their lack of substance is concealed.

Hedging is another commonplace method for avoiding a categorical answer. In effect, hedging returns to the questioner not a decisive answer but a criterion or set of criteria for arriving at a decision. To be sure, a decision-maker can be helped immeasurably by an appropriate set of criteria. The trouble with hedging is that it selects, not the most significant criteria, nor the most readily available, but the most nebulous. Anything to get off the hook. Ask a direct question and the hedger answers, "Well, it all depends. It's hard to say whether the timing will be right when we get ready. We have to make plans, get set up, and fill the pipelines. So, if you're asking whether we are doing the right thing, I suppose the answer is Yes and No. Yes if we hit it right, and No if we don't." From this barebones outline, experts at hedging can go on to construct magnificent statements that sound as though they are reaching into profound stores of knowledge. When they are in good form, it takes a bit of reflection to recognize the shallowness of their remarks. Those who learn to question the adequacy of profferred criteria are best adapted for survival. The Law of Rationalization must be their guide.

To sum up, it has often been noted that continuing things as they are implies a decision, so that one cannot really get away without making a decision altogether. Avoidance chooses by default; and delay opts for deferment. Nevertheless, *obviously* passive decisions are generally unsatisfactory for survival politics because they invite criticism. To overcome this problem, sophisticated methods have been devised for delaying decisions or doing nothing while appearing to be active. From a study of such tactics as are described above, it is plain that proper delay and inaction require planning, and specious "decisions" still require finesse. Furthermore, all these tactics risk discovery by the perceptive people in an organization—the ones who understand the Law of Rationalization, and who apply it consistently.

NEGOTIATION

Decisions involving legitimate compromise result from negotiations in which each side knows what terms it must have, what terms it is willing to yield, and what terms it will trade off in a bargaining process. A good negotiator will not openly display his willingness to make concessions too soon: Some of the points he is willing to give away may have exchange value after all. If the minimum terms of the two sides do not conflict seriously, negotiations should run smoothly.

Inexperienced negotiators often enter a meeting with no clear idea of their minimum terms. Thinking of maximum conditions only, vaguely willing to back down part way, and making a virtue of *playing it by ear*, they require time to reassess their position at every turn. No matter what the other side's tactics are, it is far better to have one's own ranges established in advance, to know what is acceptable, what is negotiable, and what will not be given up.

In order to avoid creating an appearance of stubbornness, negotiators often raise their demands at the outset, so that later they may seem to be making concessions when in fact they are not. As a counterstrategy, it helps to work out in advance an opposition list similar to one's own, comprising estimates of the minimum terms the other side will really insist on, the terms they are willing to concede, and the horse-trading they are probably prepared to engage in. Mere inflation of demands by the people on the other side should not be permitted to work in their favor.

When departments negotiate within a company, as over transfer-pricing policy or division of responsibilities, they can be expected to resolve their differences rather quickly. Power is tacitly at issue, and the negotiators know how much power has shifted since the last round. Furthermore, intransigence from any quarter will not be allowed to jeopardize the company's survival, as the Law of Group Survival makes clear.

Some negotiators present themselves as hard bargainers. They assume a tough bargaining posture from the outset, in the expectation that others will make concessions more readily to a rigid opponent than to one with a softer style. The hard bargainer lets it be known that he is not giving away anything, and he becomes indignant at the thought that his adversaries want so much from him (no matter how far they may have pared down their demands in vain attempts at appeasement).

Another bargaining tactic is to turn on the charm to soften the opposition. The charmers may appear hurt when they are denied victory on a point, and they may expect the other side to compensate on the next item. The intent is always to break the resolve of adversaries, so that they may find it in their hearts to give things away.

The two tactics—hard bargaining and charm—may be combined in one person or one bargaining team; the soft manner turns to a hard stance. In a team effort, the easygoing partner may pretend to be mollifying his obdurate associate in order to resume negotiations—after the opposition's defenses have been tested and its limits of retreat have been discovered.

One last word on negotiations and compromise. Concessions must be proper. Giving away the rights of others, without their prior consent, can vitiate a deal or cause problems when people have to be faced later. It's better to use the actual or presumed reluctance of third parties to justify unwillingness to go along with doubtful propositions. Carrying this thinking a step further, if a reluctant partner can be an asset in negotiating, imagine how much can be accomplished with a delicate concern for mysterious noncombatants (like a "silent majority")!

PREDICTION

Forecasting and estimating are kin to decision-making. Predicting the results of alternative proposals is part of the decision process. Additionally, managers are as reluctant to project into the future as they are to decide matters in the present—and for the same reason. The fear of being shown up acts as a damping influence over both activities.

However, in the forecasting field, consultants work at squeezing predictions out of the reticent. One ingenious technique gathers guesses from executives and distributes the average estimates for second-round revisions. A herd instinct brings the wild guessers closer to the average this time, and a consensus emerges. Now the perpetrators of the method, proud of their foreknowledge of group behavior, happily proclaim the success of the *Delphi technique* in promoting agreement once again. The oracle has spoken; its forecast has respectability.

Another technique for evincing estimates from individuals harasses them for extreme figures—the highest and lowest imaginable—and then reasonable highs and lows, getting each person to admit that a likely figure exists somewhere between. Caution naturally takes over, and the *likely estimate* turns up near the middle of the range. In order to provide further assurance of a solid mathematical-statistical basis, the consultants then weight the *most likely* figure by four in calculating an arithmetic mean that few would have the courage and ill grace to dispute. (For those with a mathematical bent, this mean is the sum of high, low, and four times the most likely estimate, divided by six.) The effect of this calculation is to place the final estimate even closer to the midpoint than was the crude most-likely figure. Finally, the estimates of a number of people may be averaged in the sophisticated belief that there can never be too many cooks.

With the estimates from these techniques employed as input, a great many involved calculations can be made, and computers working with *mathematical models* can bring out marvelous results. By this time, the combined joy of conception and travail of gestation is sufficient to guarantee that the results will be dearly loved by all.

So it is that forecasts are sometimes easier to make than decisions, although common sense whispers that it ought to be the other way around

13

INNOVATION AND CHANGE

INNOVATION KEEPS a company from becoming moribund. In a free-enterprise system, the company that brings out a stream of new products can stay ahead of its competitors. Similarly, new operating methods that promote efficiency are a proper manifestation of the profit motive at work. In recognition of these truisms, business leaders on the podium extol innovation while bemoaning the paucity of creative minds. In fact, however beguiling the lip-service to innovators may be, they remain the most unwelcome and mistrusted people in organizations everywhere.

The mere suggestion of an innovative approach is enough to make people run for cover. Innovation presages change, which brings uncertainty and invites turbulence. People in an organization turn the Law of Group Survival inside out, protecting themselves collectively within, instead of promoting their group's interests against outside competition. The process is reminiscent of the way in which a living organism may pervert its immunological system to reject an organ transplant that would otherwise have ensured the viability of the whole.

Hope for innovators lies in making their efforts compatible with their company's *immunological system*, much as hematologists have made blood transfusions practicable by testing specimens for compatibility. It must be recognized that an innovator is coping with a perverse reaction of a powerful natural law. Defiance of the Law of Group Survival by an individual would be too distressing to go unpunished by the organization. However, a similar perversion by the group can be overcome by an individual.

After Susan Williams began to specialize, she profited from having time to explore her subject in depth, opportunities to probe the frontiers of knowledge with colleagues, and challenges to contend with. Few sets of circumstances could have been more conducive to creativity; and Susan spawned ideas. The reaction among her peers was predictable. To hear them tell it, Susan had lost touch with reality; she flitted from one subject to another in a vain effort to escape detection. Any effort to seek amplification of Susan's ideas, they reasoned, was bound to be unrewarding.

But if rivalry blinded people at Susan's level, surely the higher echelons were not in direct competition with her. What was their problem? First, Susan upset their staffs, and that was dangerous. Second, her ideas threatened repercussions up the line, and that was disturbing. Third, her penchant for originality startled "creative" people at all levels, and they could be neither objective nor receptive toward her.

Take, for example, Susan's boss, a fairly typical self-made executive who had clawed his way up. On looking back, he chose not to recall the in-fighting that had marked his progress, but rather to embellish the ideas he had conceived (or stolen). It pleased him to attribute his success to a combination of imaginative thought, excellent judgment, and hard work. Believing in his own originality, he could sincerely lament its absence among others. His search for first-rate subordinates was really a hunt for people who "could take an idea and run with it"—guess whose idea!

For Susan, as for all innovators, there were four choices. She could go on earning her salary by performing her duties acceptably, without challenging established customs. This is the easy way out; but it would prove frustrating, unless Susan were to channel her creative impulses into extracurricular activities.

Or she could divert her energies to immediate matters of practical consequence and present herself as a person who gets things done. Since action, not ideas, is what the organization types respect, it makes sense to stress one's abilities as a doer, instead of contending with the obstacles that face a genuine thinker.

Or she could adopt a self-effacing attitude, turning over the credit to her boss or her peers and trusting to the gratitude and goodwill of these beneficiaries in their future dealings with her. In all likelihood, their memories would prove unequal to the charge. And that could actually be fortunate, because gratitude would otherwise be overwhelmed by embarrassment, and Susan would be made to pay a penalty in one form or another.

Or she could harken to the accumulated wisdom of successful management consultants who have learned to thrive amid hostility, living by their wits in organizational settings. The following sections present an adaptation of consulting lore to internal politicking for the survival of the innovative personality.

A PROTOCOL FOR CHANGE

Since a Natural Law—the Law of Group Survival—has gone awry, the innovator must contemplate a strategy which would be foolhardy under other circumstances, but is now only risky. She must go over the heads of her boss, his boss, and so on, right to the top of the pyramid. Sponsorship for true innovation will generally come only from on high. Indeed, it would be better still to go behind the scenes to the sources of power, if that is possible.

Innovators are playing for high stakes. Others know that, even if the creative ones sometimes blind themselves to the realities of the game. On entering the contest, the innovator's best bet is to put all her chips down and gamble for the big win, instead of watching her stack of chips dwindle as she loses a series of side bets in a vain quest for paltry gains. Attempts to establish a reputation for creativity at lower levels can only bring undesirable results: schemers stealing one's ideas; opponents bombarding one's suggestions or side-tracking one's proposals; and rivals launching veiled personal attacks.

In the face of the poor odds associated with adherence to the chain of command, an assault on the organization chart, vaulting directly to the top, takes on the aspect of an acceptable, or rather an unavoidable, risk. With preparation and persistence, it is often possible to carry off such a strategy. If impenetrable barriers are interposed, however, and persistence is unavailing, then it's time to move on to another company whose structure and receptivity to new ideas may be more encouraging.

The first goal is to get a hearing at the top. Presenting her own case is an innovator's first prerogative, and one that she ought never to relinquish. No one else has her familiarity with or understanding of the subject. No one else has her interest in getting the message across. No one else will protect her stake in the outcome. She must carry the word to the top herself.

The Proposal. After interest in the project has been awakened, the next step is to prepare and deliver a proposal. At this point, the innovator presents a reasonably strong case for a study, marshaling facts uncovered by her preliminary work and withholding much additional information with which to counter opposition. The best approach is one that answers for each listener the question, "What's in it for me?" Not only benefits to the company must be spelled out, but also benefits to decision-makers as individuals.

Others will want to steal the project, claiming all the while that the innovator is usurping their authority, that she is unaware of many issues and their ramifications, and that she needs their guidance. (Incidentally, on the other side of the fence, similar claims form a good basic position for people threatened by a meddler.) Defensive managers will also produce fragments of studies to show that they have been approaching the same subject with methods that offer better prospects for success. If an operating manager hollers loudly, he will probably be assigned the project himself, and the innovator will have to be content with an acknowledgment of her role in getting it underway. Even that recognition may represent a gain of sorts: Outright opposition could have been more difficult to handle.

If possible, a proposal should be segmented into phases, to be undertaken one at a time. There is much to be gained from this approach. The first phase can be limited to a modest commitment of resources. Moreover, premature attacks on the whole project can be forestalled by putting off many subjects for future debate in connection with later phases. The entire proposal may be too much for small minds to grasp all at once; but one phase is more easily explained and defended from arbitrary assaults. If the proposal is accepted, the end of each phase will become a reporting milestone for progress reports to management and for reassessing future plans in the light of experience acquired.

Reporting. Progress should be reported regularly to the sponsor. The most useful reporting method is to set before the sponsor a painstakingly edited report clearly marked *Rough Draft*. He need not be told that this report before him is the best the innovator is capable of. As innovator and sponsor read the draft together, the fiction is maintained that the report is merely an early draft, ready for nothing more than previewing.

The draft has, of course, incorporated suggestions from all available sources. Loopholes have been plugged and uncertainties resolved. Nevertheless, the sponsor may have comments of his own to add. These are noted for elaboration and inclusion in the next draft. The more the sponsor is encouraged to join in the preparation of a report, the more likely he is to take a proprietary interest in the result.

Is it really necessary to observe the formalities of offering a proposal and following up with reports? By all means. It is even better to present the final report, with visual aids, to a group of executives. Remember always that the importance of a project is measured, not by its cost/benefit ratio, its effect on the organization, or even the bottom-line result, as is often supposed, but rather by the level of sponsorship and the fuss that innovator and sponsor make over the results. From a distance an orange balloon looks much like a pumpkin, except that one is filled with nourishment and the other with gas. Few executives can discriminate between them.

The initiating proposal is necessary, too. A simple report at the outset, in place of a proposal, would almost certainly draw a *That needs more work* response from others, as a device for taking over the project. A cry would go up that a workable transmutation might come out of the efforts of more experienced people coming to the rescue.

A second thieving stratagem introduces a string of modifications, elaborately presented and followed by a series of releases aimed at associating the project, in people's minds, with the author of the revisions. The originator's contribution is often quite forgotten.

A third ploy purports to have discovered omissions. It is often possible to extend ideas into areas that were not touched on, or not fully explored, in the original report. By extending the proposal, someone can display his analytical mind through warnings of lost opportunities and near-disasters. Once again, the innovator is faced with losing her project to more seasoned hands.

Implementation. After a recommendation for change has been reported and accepted, the project can still be defeated during the *implementation* stage, when the operating people have their final fling. If the innovator is a line manager, then she should supervise the implementation of her own ideas in her own activity; a staff innovator can only advise the line, being careful not to impinge upon the authority vested in others. This division of responsibility makes for some interesting situations.

Here's the picture as perceived by a line manager: "A rash —though perhaps bright—staff person has recommended changes in a department with whose operations she has only the barest familiarity. By rushing past the chain of command, she has somehow charmed top management—who can't know everything that goes on—into accepting her untried schemes. Now I have to keep my people in line to make an outsider's half-baked ideas work. We'll see."

This situation recurs often enough for management consultants to have developed prescriptions for *the management of change.* Basically, the remedies comprise communication, participation, and support. As for support, the need is to get top management behind the project, visibly and vocally, so that open resistance will not be tolerated. Since obstructionists will operate underhandedly in any case, support from above can be employed effectively only by patiently ferreting out every act of sabotage, until the threat of retribution becomes reality.

Communication and participation are discussed more fully in other chapters. In regard to implementing change, open communication may not be as efficacious as is sometimes supposed. Theoretical explanations confuse many people, especially when they project too far into the future. Immediate, practical training is more effective, both in teaching and in motivating.

As for participative management in effecting change, it is virtually precluded by the fact that a recommendation has already been adopted by higher management. At this point, attempts to convince employees that they are participating to a significant degree in the planning of changes will not work. It's better to hand down the new procedures forthrightly and offer help in coping with the challenges they impose.

Is there no way to alleviate the suffering of those who are caught in an upheaval? Look at it this way: they bring much of their tribulation on themselves. The important thing is not to get caught up in their problems:

• Don't try to rescue a line manager by intimating that he was instrumental in getting changes adopted. His subordinates enjoy his discomfort at having new procedures imposed on him. They'll turn against him otherwise.

• Don't issue orders to line people. If they resist, you'll be in trouble; let their boss tell them what to do. Let him worry.

• Don't let the envy or the self-pity of the line people affect you. It's better that you succeed and they remain envious than that they win and you suffer frustration.

• Don't let self-justification by the line delay or modify your plans. Insist on relevance whenever a suggestion or complaint arises.

• When a reduction of staff is necessary, don't fall for the *attrition* artifice, which either the personnel people or the line managers may suggest. (Remind them, if necessary, that attrition involves rubbing away by friction, not waiting for people to leave voluntarily.) In practice, hanging on to redundant employees encourages make-work projects and prolongs feelings of insecurity. The productive people will be happier to count themselves among the survivors of a house-

• Act businesslike and methodical. See that the job gets cleaning perpetrated in a single deft blow.
done right; then get out.

• Write your own final report to ensure that your success is neither minimized by depreciation and irrelevancies nor attributed to less deserving people than yourself.

MANAGING AN INNOVATOR

The previous discussion was addressed to innovators. A word remains to be said to the manager who finds an innovator on his hands. George Roberts was in that position. One of his people brought him ideas for improving matters. She should have gone to the top, of course, but she went to her boss instead.

George seized the opportunity to get into the act, so that he became a co-author of the proposal. Nevertheless, he still felt that the project would benefit his subordinate more than himself. Accordingly, he was reluctant to expose himself to the added risks of reaching for the top on his own. He played the organization game instead, thus giving his own boss a chance to further dilute authorship. In the end, nobody got much credit; but then again, the final version of the recommendations, as implemented, wasn't worth very much to the company anyhow.

Arthur Gordon is in a different position. When anyone comes to him with an idea, he ushers the innovator next door—into the president's office—contenting himself with the role of midwife. Word having gotten around, Arthur's obstetrical services are called on quite often, to the advantage of Arthur and the innovators who come to him—and to the consternation of others in the organization.

Company presidents often proclaim an open-door policy. When there is no Arthur Gordon around to lead the way, such a policy will abet the innovator reaching for the top. On the other hand, bringing grievances through the open door is unwise. Remember that disregard for the organization chart is a serious matter entailing grave risks. Such a thought may be entertained as a possible recourse only when the potential reward is commensurate with the risk. For innovation, yes; for complaints, no.

V

COMMUNICATION
AND
INTERACTION

14

GARBLED
COMMUNICATIONS

IN THE ARGOT of management consultants, a favorite
buzz word is *communications*. Starting with *verbal* (speaking
and writing), the term has expanded to include *nonverbal*
(facial expression, body language, and timing). Each mode of
expression—speaking, writing, and signaling—has its counterpart: listening, reading, and observing. Additionally, separate
categories exist for public and private, formal and informal,
face-to-face and distant (or impersonal) communication.
Theories have been developed to cover *languages, techniques,
carriers,* and *networks*. From the technology of electronic
communication, the behavioral side of communicating has
borrowed and extended such terms as *transmitting, receiving,
noise, interference,* and *feedback*. All of this is interesting,
and important in its place. However, for our purposes it is
sufficient to note the buzz words in passing and to move on
to the political overtones of informational exchanges.

The story of the Tower of Babel accounts for a multi-
plicity of tongues as God's instrument for keeping mankind
in place. "One people with one language" became arrogant,

so God confounded their speech, rendering them incapable of working together.

Today, Babel has lost its cogency as a moral lesson on arrogance. Men and women who have watched astronauts on the moon may be forgiven if they regard a great tower as a quaintly charming relic of a less sophisticated past. But the present-day concern with communication allows the story of Babel to be reinterpreted as a communications breakdown that management consultants can understand and deplore.

INTELLIGENCE-GATHERING

The customary assessment of communications misses the mark when it ascribes failures to sheer ignorance. To account thus for all the lapses that occur would imply widespread ineptitude of mammoth proportions. No, the causes of garbling must be sought primarily in premeditated acts of obfuscation, intended primarily to thwart inquisitive people and organizations.

Governments and companies practice espionage in varying degrees, depending on the morals of the management, the alertness of the outside world, and the tolerance of society. Spies are planted, secrets are stolen, telephones are bugged, agents are corrupted. Assuredly, these tactics are regarded with distrust—chiefly because they run risks of exposure which might result in legal action, bad publicity, or countermeasures. However, questionable methods continue to be employed.

An individual needs information, updated continuously, and an ability to detect and interpret warning signals. Optimum timing for a switch to a winning side demands inside information. Furthermore, it is always necessary to sort out people, to conjecture who is on which side, and to divine how strong their loyalties are. For all these purposes, there is nothing as comforting as reliable information.

Much information can be garnered directly, by keeping in

touch with others. When prospective sources are at a distance away, frequent telephone calls, visits, and lunches are in order, using pretexts, if necessary. In a company with scattered operations, some traveling is called for. Travelers have more opportunities to pick up stray bits of information than the office-bound types. In addition, the personal relations that are maintained by frequent contact could one day turn out to be almost as valuable as the information that is swapped.

The individual's primary source of information is, of course, the grapevine (in formal nomenclature, the informal network). Hooking into a network takes time, but the effort to gain acceptance is worthwhile, for members have a right to expect prompt information on a wide variety of politically opportune subjects. Informal networks have always been a major barrier for outsiders from minority groups. But the willingness of today's young people to tear down these barriers is a hopeful sign for civilization—and one that thought-leaders among the older generation deserve some credit for having fostered.

Since planted stories abound (the equivalent of *interference* on a television set), unfounded rumors may be picked up at random (like *noise* on the audio), and distortions can develop in passing data along (as from poor tuning of a receiver). All information must be held suspect until confirmed. The confirmation process may be difficult, because one could be hearing from three different people a story that traces back to a single source. Despite such uncertainties, corroboration must be sought.

Information-gathering suffers from a great many handicaps. To begin with, companies do not communicate accurately. They deliberately conceal and confuse. Immortals in mythology have always exercised prerogatives denied to humans. Perhaps the modern corporation, having been invested with immortality, is only following the example of the less honorable Olympian gods.

At the most elementary level, companies offer the façade that suits their purpose best. Obeying the Law of Self-Interest, corporations, in their financial reports, grin through adversity, stoutly maintaining either that all is well or that the worst is over, and conditions are expected to improve. Meanwhile, other companies may cry poormouth. A utility pleads for a rate increase on the grounds that it can't make ends meet now and replace wornout equipment in the distant future, too. Oil companies insist they must be given depletion allowances to encourage them to explore for new wells. There's little harm in all this posturing, because few people take it seriously. Generally, since companies deliberately broadcast interference, their pronouncements require corroboration before they can be trusted.

Similarly, in dealing with people inside the company, the Law of Rationalization suggests the wisdom of a practiced wariness. In ordinary conversation, guileless people distort facts as they repeat them, and schemers intentionally introduce false signals. Along with the need to remain alert to goings-on, and the need to adapt quickly to fluid situations, survival demands prudent caution. Once again, stories must be corroborated. The gullible suffer as much as the uninformed.

Skepticism leads to questioning: First, how reliable is the source? In logic, the argumentum ad hominem is considered a fallacy: The validity of a proposition is not to be doubted merely because it comes from a doubtful source. In a pragmatic situation, however, the doubtfulness of the source is a symptom that must not be discarded casually. And politics is pragmatic.

Second, does the story ring true? Is its reasonableness tinged with just enough irony to be judged realistic? A tale that is too pat should arouse suspicion. It is more likely to have been contrived than the story that has some loose ends or some fuzzy edges.

Third, and most important of all, who stands to gain?

This is the ancient touchstone of *cui bono*—to whose good? If general acceptance of an item of information could benefit someone in particular, then he becomes a prime suspect. He could have put the rumor into circulation.

An extension of *cui bono* is a prime investigatory tool: Who might be able to put himself or another in a position to benefit? Few guides are more useful in directing the search for hidden culprits. Whenever an individual senses that something is amiss, he must enumerate, not his own possible failings or peccadillos—for they are irrelevant—but the people who may want to do him harm. In many situations, it is impossible for one person to keep track of all the hidden problem-sources; hence, a direct indicator of potential trouble-makers is most useful. The most serviceable indicator by far is *cui bono*. Who might want to create an opening for a relative who needs a job, or a good friend to whom a favor is due? The test of *cui bono* brings the chief suspects into focus. Furthermore, since only the sources of power and their agents have real influence, the search can be narrowed once again to manageable proportions by adding PFM to *cui bono*: Who among the sources of money stands to gain?

Often, in anticipating promotions and firings, it's helpful to watch certain weathervanes. The people who decide on personnel actions generally remain poker-faced, but others who get advance information may not be quite so adept at concealment. Some of them may be just a bit more friendly or obsequious toward a person about to be promoted, and a little more aloof toward someone headed for trouble. Others overcompensate in their efforts at confounding, and only the strangeness of their behavior, not its specific content, becomes important. However, in watching for subtle signs of impending actions, one must not become overly sensitive or overtly suspicious. It does no good to panic every time a person's behavior pattern alters. She may have other things on her mind.

OPINIONS AND EVALUATIONS

To skepticism must be added awareness, in a proper recipe for survival. As companies and individuals pry, and as they parry each other's thrusts, all other persons who want to survive must also be alert to the thrusts and prepared for the challenges. A few common situations will demonstrate techniques of political communication, good and bad.

Some questions are two-pronged, in that they are aimed at the respondent himself as well as the information he provides. Such a question is, "How is So-and-so doing?" If So-and-so is a new employee, the question is normal—but often premature. He or she should be given a chance to learn the job and settle into it before anyone is made to go out on a limb with an evaluation. But if So-and-so has been around awhile, there is reason for exceptional caution. Some personnel action may be in the offing, perhaps a promotion or a dismissal—and the respondent frequently doesn't know which. Arthur Gordon is fully aware that the assessments he makes, whether of persons, books, stocks, procedures, or proposals, become matters on which his judgment will be evaluated by others. For that reason, it's hard for anyone to catch him announcing an offhand opinion, a tentative conclusion, or a vague impression. "What Peter says about Paul tells more about Peter than it does about Paul."

All judgments are risky, but premature evaluations are the riskiest by far. To find that an original assessment was wrong would impale Arthur on the horns of a dilemma. To admit such mistakes creates an image of unreliability. Apparent uncertainty makes others ill at ease, especially when they are in a fault-finding mood. On the other hand, holding fast to a mistake runs risks of double exposure—for the mistake itself and for showing unfairness.

Nevertheless, the company president asks, "How is So-and-so doing?" and he is in a position to demand an answer.

He'll press until he gets one. What does Arthur do now?

First, he includes a factual statement in his reply, to make clear the limitations of his assessment. "So-and-so's assignment is to adapt operational auditing techniques to our company's needs. Her progress to date is satisfactory" (or slow, or whatever). "So-and-so directed the study on eating habits in the company cafeteria. Her time was about right, considering that she was new to that sort of work (or to her surroundings); and her conclusions looked reasonable enough" (or disappointing, perhaps).

Second, he prepares for evaluations by keeping a diary of significant information, and by reviewing his records periodically, asking himself repeatedly the inevitable question, "How is So-and-so doing?" He also keeps records of opinions he has expressed to others.

Third, when his opinion changes, Arthur finds an appropriate reason to account for the improvement or deterioration in So-and-so's performance. Improvement is subtly attributed to Arthur's guidance, whereas deterioration may be traceable to So-and-so's recent personal problems, or her flash-in-the-pan characteristics: She undertakes new projects with enthusiasm and vigor, but then the fireball burns out.

In any case, mere leniency in evaluating people will not avoid trouble. Softness is not considered a virtue, but excessive harshness won't work, either. It's hard enough to get raises for people, without having previously disparaged their efforts. (Arthur refuses to resort to the stale *giving them encouragement* routine.) Responses to the question "How is So-and-so doing?" should exude integrity, bespeak fairness, proclaim prudent caution, and engender confidence.

Akin to "How is So-and-so doing?" is the seemingly innocuous request for an opinion on a subject one has had no time to explore. Be doubly wary if there is reason to suspect that essential information has been withheld. People often give opinions ostensibly *off the top of the head,* and one may be tempted to follow suit. Don't! Don't believe that others have neglected to explore their subject before speaking out. Executives and aspiring junior managers alike are constantly being evaluated for the judgment they show. To talk with insufficient knowledge is itself a display of poor judgment. To allow oneself to be led into an untenable position can be more than just embarrassing: It can be devastating.

Arthur has found it necessary to work out a defense against trappers. First, determined to make no statement without supporting facts, he will stall for time, if he needs it. Second, he disclaims special knowledge of the subject, whether the disclaimer is accurate or not. Third, if facts turn up subsequently that were known to the questioner all along, Arthur labels him a trapper and doubles his own guard in future dealings.

WILLFUL DISTORTION

Communications often suffer from inferior politicians who delude themselves into believing that dodges, sly misrepresentation, camouflage, and misleading ambiguity are somehow less reprehensible than outright lies. Perhaps they hope that artful dissembling is harder to uncover or to pin down. In fact, audiences don't ordinarily distinguish between specific kinds of duplicity. The considerable effort needed for competent dissembling would be better spent in finding a way to make the simple truth tolerable to those who are injured by it. An honest explanation need not be brutal, and though it may fail to win support, it can earn respect; whereas dissembling, once exposed, must inevitably lose on both counts. Liars have their problems, especially when they have to deal with the same unforgiving people over a long period.

Some people specialize in carrying tales. Anyone who readily tells you the current gossip being circulated behind your back is probably an instigator. Knowing that such reports must be diluted with liberal quantities of skepticism, Susan Williams is not one to snap at baited hooks. She prefers to reflect that they are undoubtedly accorded the same chary reception elsewhere that she gives the stories she hears about others. There is no need for her to issue denials.

When real trouble develops, and there is cause to suspect ill-will, Susan is slow to accuse others. Misunderstandings arise in myriad ways, some of them innocent. After all, speaker and listener are different people with different points of view and preoccupations, and even seemingly simple requests can be misinterpreted.

Nevertheless, some misunderstandings have an extraordinarily suspicious look to them. Thus, one wonders whether the people in the mail room put airmail stamps on interoffice memoranda because they were rushed, or because they're incompetent, or because they were inclined toward mischievous behavior. It's quite possible that they acted deliberately, out of pique. If that is the case, then it's time to consider whether petty annoyances may be avoided by simply being pleasant. Some troublemakers are only looking for a kind word, an occasional expression of gratitude, or some recognition as individuals. The Law of Fugling requires gracious conduct, even toward offenders.

Few people are sufficiently lacking in moral scruples to pursue a *big lie* technique, but those few can stir up more mischief than honest people can handle. Most often, fabricators follow a pattern of adhering to actual occurrences within their experience and switching roles so that they look good and their victims look bad. Adept at weaving a plot, fabricators will embellish their stories with details which lend a specious air of realism.

Overcoming the damage done by a well-constructed lie, whose details are apparently in order, is difficult. One defense is to keep everything of political consequence documented and reported routinely. Defending against charges afterward is less effective, if indeed the opportunity ever arises. (Creating such opportunities is, of course, a legitimate goal of politicking.) It may be of some comfort that fabricators eventually acquire unsavory reputations. Once their credibility is tarnished, they can do little harm—and credibility comes under close scrutiny more frequently these days.

An ancient ploy, *divide and rule* requires concealment, especially when used in a modern, sophisticated setting. Although openness tends to diminish the threat of the dividers, the strategy remains a dangerous influence, threatening to split groups or turn them against each other. Tale-bearers are divisive, whether their stories are true or not, and whether their material is scandalous, inflammatory, belittling, or cautionary. On the surface, information may be passed on with seeming innocence—perhaps with humor, reluctance, or spontaneity. Some remarks may be dropped casually or "accidentally." The technique says less than the destructiveness of the content about the underlying intention of the speaker. The immediate informant may be quoting other sources. That doesn't exonerate him, but it may incriminate them, if the quotations are correct.

Another sign of divisive tendencies at work is an indication that people are being pitted against each other in an excess of competitive zeal. At all levels, up to corporate presidents, there are people who do not shrink from creating dissension in their own operations. In Susan Williams's company, the owner himself was a chief offender! It may be charitable to assume that everyone's intentions are good, but it is more politic to distrust those who spur competition beyond reasonable limits.

Alerting one's grapevine to a troublemaker's activities is essential to group and self-preservation. People in a network should discuss rumors freely, risking confrontations among themselves, if necessary, rather than let fires smolder. The precise defense depends on one's level, but it always involves a healthy skepticism and a refusal to transmit gossip.

TERGIVERSATION

"How do you adjust this chair?" someone asked, and before George Roberts could show her, a response from another source flooded him out.

"Don't do it. Don't even try. Adjusting one of those chairs is a complicated procedure that takes years to learn. Work on simpler models before you take on an intricate design that adjusts to posture and height. Some people have been adjusting chairs for years, and all they know is that you turn a couple of wheels. They don't realize that the invention of the wheel itself was a milestone in the history of civilization. And this isn't just any old wheel. It adjusts a screw mechanism, which was another great contribution to engineering; there are mathematical textbooks on the theory of screws. And that isn't the whole story. There's a spring that's a study in itself; it took centuries to develop the materials to the right degree of elasticity. It can take days to adjust a chair properly. Another thing: Don't let the boss catch you adjusting a chair. He won't say anything, but he'll remember; and next thing you'll have problems without knowing why. This is for your own good. I'm trying to keep you out of trouble."

The word *tergiversation* has two meanings: the turning away from where one's loyalties presumably have been; and the deserting of a straightforward course by dodging and prevaricating. Ask a tergiversator a simple question and you get an interminable stream of irrelevancies in return. If the question is important to your job, you may have to go elsewhere for help.

Is the tergiversator merely a long-winded fool? By no means! He is, in fact, a highly competent specialist at withholding information. Every question put to him will become the occasion for a fresh torrent of words, until his gibberish induces an urge to scream or commit mayhem. Neither act will avail, because tergiversators are generally self-controlled and well entrenched. Pressing the inquiry in oral conversation won't help much, either. These people never tire of repeating the same wearisome answers in the same words. In a war of attrition, they are indefatigable.

When they want to, tergiversators are very well able to supply direct answers. Let the question of adjusting chairs come up in the presence of an executive (admittedly an improbable illustration, but it serves to make a point), and with alacrity and aplomb, the tergiversator will proceed to demonstrate exactly what to do, without waste of words or actions, while his earlier victim is left in open-mouthed wonder. Indeed, she will be lucky if the demonstration cuts her off before she spouts the tergiversator's nonsense.

To avoid turning a tergiversator loose on newcomers to his staff, George Roberts arranged meetings in his office, where he could listen in on the explanations that were given. His presence had a wholesome effect. However, he sometimes had problems with tergiversators from other departments, generally people at his own level. In those instances, George asked for written procedures, often sitting with other persons and taking notes that were later transcribed into crude procedures, which the interviewees were asked to corroborate and sign. Then, as George worked things out for himself, no tergiversator could make capital of mistakes caused by omissions and ambiguities in the written procedures—or by noncooperation.

15

OVERCOMING THE NOISE BARRIER

THE LAW OF AGGRANDIZEMENT tells one that, in an organized effort of any sort, others will be seeking an advantage over him. Hence, preparations must be made to counter people's politicking.

Whether it be competition, dishonesty, or corruption, for every style of aggression there is a defense. This chapter will explore defenses related to communication. Whereas the previous chapter looked into the garbling of communications, this chapter will turn toward communicating for survival.

First let it be noted that communicating begins with appearances. The presence expected of a leader—which includes manner and bearing—is essential. Most important are a dedicated mien and a confident aura. Whether one actually feels dedicated and confident is irrelevant.

THE IMPORTANCE OF BEING HEARD

Having established a suitable appearance, one must concentrate next on being articulate. Assuredly, it is useful to be known as a good listener, and both the fact and the reputation can serve one well—but not well enough. The Law of Fugling demands graceful self-expression, too. Those who do the most talking about the value of listening are the ones who do the most talking, for they are most in need of good listeners.

Few people have a genuine taste for conflict, and many harbor a fear that expressing an opinion might lead to a confrontation. Others dread being proved wrong and having to retract an erroneous statement; so they are cautious beyond the bounds of prudence, agonizing over small matters and hedging their comments. Intellectual doubt is all the more unfortunate in business when meticulous habits of speech convey diffidence instead of care. Remember, uncertainty of expression reduces credibility with a typical audience. The result can be tragic when fear of rejection is reinforced by failure to convince others. So it is that some highly competent persons characteristically maintain a posture of silence when they might otherwise contribute significantly to an intelligent dialogue. To be sure, *leaders generally come from the ranks of the doers; but the articulate doers are odds-on favorites.* The quiet ones may be denied the chance to act in the first place. So it becomes essential to make yourself heard—and read, too. Learning to write well takes time and effort, but successful politicking requires such an investment. In politicking, a person's chief weapons, for offense and defense, are tongue and pen.

BUSINESS WRITING AND SPEAKING

Your co-workers' writing is a valuable key to your judgment of them. By the same token, your own writing should reflect your competence and personality. Before exposing your thoughts to others, cleanse them of meanness, pettiness, or bias. And work at expressing yourself precisely, for that is the only way to avoid being misinterpreted.

The fundamental units of writing are words and sentences. Begin with them. Dictionaries and usage books are invaluable in achieving precision, whereas how-to books are not uniformly good. In fact, those theories of writing that fail to recognize the trade-off between readability and precision are quite dangerous.

The trade-off exists. An utterly precise statement that includes limits, exceptions, modifications, and provisos becomes unreadable. It is meant to be pored over as a reference. Regulations and procedures are not intended for reading enjoyment. For some purposes, readability must be sacrificed.

Even when readability remains a legitimate goal, it should not be attempted by way of the short-short-short shibboleth: short words, short sentences, short paragraphs. Actually, the short word is not automatically the correct one to convey your meaning; the precise word is always the one to use. (Whereas precise statements may become unreadable, precise words do not.) Nor is a series of short sentences the best vehicle for carrying a complex thought; a complex sentence will do the job better. And chopping up paragraphs to shorten them artificially is a devilish device for confounding readers. Each idea needs to be developed, and the paragraph ends only when that development is complete.

The reader-oriented approach makes better sense. Analogous to market-orientation among salespersons, this approach directs the appeal, the style, and the vocabulary toward the reader. The assumptions that are made are the ones that an analysis of the audience's wants and needs dictates. However, the conclusions are not necessarily those that the audience wants to hear: The reader-oriented approach does not pander. It picks up the reader where he is and carries him to where the writer wants him to be (which again requires subtlety). When editing, inculcate reader-orientation among your staff. If a draft is insensitive to readers' interests, there's no harm in asking the writer how he thinks another person will react to his suggestions.

The catch in the reader-oriented approach is that few pieces of business writing are seen by one reader alone. Even the full list of addressees on a report does not always encompass the whole range of readers; others will come by the report in the normal course of business. Frequently, the best one can do is to accommodate one's writing to a reasonable range of education, background, and interests, subtly working in facts that some potential readers need and others know.

In business writing, a balance must be maintained between the general and the specific. A mere statement of opinion without supporting data is likely to get nowhere with business readers. They will look upon generalities as fuzzy. However, an enumeration of fragmented details, without benefit of a unifying cover, throws the burden of analysis over to potentially unwilling readers. Since business writing should establish a point, it is the writer's duty to set forth that point clearly, for all to follow. In short, a combination of general and particular, of details and summaries, of concepts and concrete illustrations, is a requisite for good business writing.

There are, of course, many similarities between speaking and writing, and many differences. Although much of the previous discussion of writing applies with equal force to speaking, some additional comments will be helpful to speakers. Short words and short sentences are more welcome to a listener than to a careful reader; and restatements can make up for what is lost. Immediate listener response also helps the speaker.

Repetition is appropriate, especially in formal speaking. Listeners wander and get lost; frequent recapitulation helps to bring them back. Additionally, repetition helps to get novel or complex thoughts across. The shock is less severe on a second hearing; and the mind-set has been altered by the initial assault.

Whereas variety in writing is achieved by style, variety in

speaking may be accomplished in the delivery. Voice-modulation, changes in tempo, pauses, and question periods can do for the speaker what writing skill alone must do for the writer.

Informal or conversational speech requires mastery, too. Having a store of subjects on which to hold one's own is helpful, of course. Additionally, practice brings expertise. And there is a substantial transfer of skill between modes of communication. Every step taken to improve your delivery on the speaker's platform will help your delivery elsewhere, and vice versa. As your command of the English language improves, so will your fugling.

STRATEGIES FOR COMMUNICATING

Regrettably, despite your best efforts to communicate well with others and see things as others see them, misunderstandings develop—and some of them are genuine. When that happens, someone may offer to straighten out differences and restore harmonious relations. At times, it is necessary to rely on another person to do what one is unable to accomplish alone.

It is best to act on one's own, but if the help of others must be sought, or if an offer of assistance cannot be turned away, you must still do your part. It's dangerous to leave to others the working out of your own problems. Without impugning anyone's motives, recognize that the intermediaries will be working to their own advantage. You still may come out ahead, but your interests will become a secondary consideration.

On finding herself under attack, Susan looks for ways to tell her side of the story, and she readies her case. Of the many ways to present a defense—orally or in writing, formally or informally—it is most important to be ready for brief, spontaneous, oral statements as opportunities arise.

To do that, Susan acquires a good grasp of the line of reasoning she selects, virtually forsaking other possible arguments; she becomes well versed in the significant parts, stripped of nonessential details; and she is ready to sound practical rather than theoretical. There is no point in talking about "too large a span of control"; even those who are familiar with management terminology will shrink from such jargon. Susan says simply that the supervisors are spread too thin.

Susan has to expect misrepresentation by others, but there is no need to prepare for every eventuality. When a real shocker comes, she can note that certain statements don't jibe with the facts as she knows them, and she can promise to ascertain where the truth lies. Verification of the facts cannot, of course, be entrusted to others. Opponents have already slanted and distorted issues; and not-so-disinterested third parties may be swayed by political considerations.

Although dismantling the opposition's case is effective, it is desirable to build an affirmative offense as well. When George Roberts became production manager, he had to defend his domain. The systems people suggested removing the warehouse operation from George and combining it with the shipping department under the sales manager. George gathered his own data and proceeded to demonstrate that raw materials and subassemblies were handled by the warehouse crew. He also took immediate measures to tighten the links between the warehouse and the factory. Thereafter, George could argue his case from a position of strength.

George is also a clever fighter in that he moderates his attack. To begin with, he acknowledges the arguments of the other side. By that action, he not only demonstrates an awareness of opposing views, but he also proclaims his open-mindedness. It would be difficult thereafter for anyone to portray him as a zealot. George's statement of both sides is often aimed at opening the opposition case prematurely and in unfavorable circumstances. Stating the other side's position early and fairly—an appearance of fairness is essential if one's answers are to stand up—can be a useful ploy: When opponents present their arguments later, they will no longer be fresh and new.

Attribution of remarks to others can serve several purposes, depending on the circumstances. Responsibility for a doubtful assertion is avoided by quoting the source; giving credit for a genuine contribution can earn someone's gratitude. In any case, an attributed statement, accompanied by neutral or balanced comments, can serve as a trial balloon, without committing oneself to a position.

Loopholes and weasel words are not nearly as effective as many people suppose. Their purpose is immediately transparent to a sophisticated audience; and danger lurks in the possibility of arousing suspicion. Certainly, anyone who undertakes to do something risky is entitled to insert reasonable provisos in his agreements, but broad, ill-concealed escape hatches are unwarranted.

When someone else is being vague in his presentation, it is often good strategy to ask for an illustration of his meaning: "You have recommended a reorganization. Could you indicate what specific changes you would make?" When someone is caught in a bluff, there are many polite ways to insist that he *put up or shut up.*

Humor can be an effective weapon, in its proper place. Susan Williams is the target of a determined little band that opposes her every move as an officer in a community association. At board meetings, she fights back, but meetings of the full membership pose a different sort of problem. The typical member knows little, and cares less, about in-fighting among the officers; and there's no telling how things would go for Susan in the end, if she were to take her case before the members. So she plays it safe. Her typed report is reproduced for distribution at each meeting; and its high quality bespeaks a job well done. But her oral report is something else. By the time she finishes entertaining her audience with jokes and stories, a board member wouldn't dare to take her on in open combat.

Humor can also ease tensions when compromise is blocked by hardened positions. Even if no one is able to laugh, the effort will not be a total loss. Sometimes it's helpful simply to break the pattern that a meeting has settled into.

Wit and banter are another matter, especially when barbs are directed at an individual. No one likes to be exposed to such attacks himself, even "good-naturedly," and few people relish watching others suffer embarrassment. Sarcasm is even more quickly resented by an audience, and too easily overdone by its devotees. In addition, it risks misunderstandings. Handle sarcasm with great care, and avoid irony altogether. To be effective, irony requires an in-group that knows exactly what is meant and an out-group that doesn't know. In such a situation, misunderstandings are almost certain to occur among people who might otherwise have supported your position.

16

INTEROFFICE
MEMORANDA

ONCE UPON A TIME, an ambitious young couple set out into the world to seek their fortune, and by chance they purchased an egg farm. They repaired and painted the chicken coops, fed the chickens, collected eggs, and brought them to market. But one thing the couple had not counted on: They found themselves cleaning out the coops daily and shoveling fresh chicken dung onto a large, growing, and foul-smelling heap. In time, the couple grew accustomed to their other chores, but chicken dung became an obsession with them. Finally, the couple reached the point where they lost sight of their original purpose; and when the census-taker came and asked what business they were in, they no longer thought of their occupation as egg farming and they answered that they were running a chicken-dung operation.

Goal-substitution—losing sight of proper ends, and substituting either by-products or means as ends in themselves—has long been a subject for philosophers and writers. Little wonder, then, that so many people in business get caught up in paperwork until they see it as an end in itself. Reports are prepared for everything, and they're followed by analyses, which are then interpreted and commented on. No matter how much a system has been weighted down with paperwork, an imaginative improviser can always find something new to add.

As a patriotic gesture toward helping the national economy by increasing productivity and eliminating waste, reasonable people ought to enlist in a war against paperwork. Since all memoranda, letters, and reports tend to spawn additional paperwork, there ought to be an occasional review of the reporting system, even at the risk of generating reports of the review itself. When a memorandum comes along, set it aside for a week before deciding whether to answer. And if your company should become a veritable chicken farm, keep an eye on the egg basket, lest you find yourself knee deep in chicken dung.

ANALYZING A MEMORANDUM

The ubiquitous interoffice memorandum is a study in itself. George Roberts, having developed an awareness of the political implications of memos, routinely follows a number of steps when he finds one in his mail. He begins with general preliminaries that must be considered first and reconsidered later:

- *The Subject:* Is it new or a followup?
- *The Sender:* Why did this memo come from him? In sending it, is he usurping someone else's authority? Is he trying to extend his influence? Is anyone else threatened thereby?
- *The Principal Addressees:* Why them? Is there anything unusual about the list? Do the names follow a pattern? Is someone included who doesn't *belong*?
- *The Secondary, Copied-In Recipients:* Why were they

included? Is the memo intended primarily for one or more of them? Is the memo intended to embarrass the principal addressee?

George follows these general preliminaries with a list of specific preliminaries, which are also repeated later, when the memo's contents are under detailed study:

• If George is the principal addressee, why were copies sent to, say, his boss and his chief rival? If the subject lies in a sensitive area, the sender may be hostile.

• If George is only copied in, why wasn't he a principal addressee instead? Are his prerogatives under attack?

• Does the date indicate that George's copy was delayed? If there is an advantage in early warning, why didn't the network tell George what was in the works? Is there any reason to act quickly, perhaps in order to recapture the initiative?

Having tentatively covered these preliminary considerations, George proceeds to the contents of the memorandum, asking such questions as these:

• Is the tone friendly or hostile? In either case, what inferences can be drawn?

• What is the surface message? Is it worth bothering about?

• What are the hidden messages, and what do they reveal?

To clarify that last point, the analysis of a sample memorandum follows. It was written by Melvin C., at the home office, to Harry T., at a plant, while George Roberts was involved in systems work.

INTEROFFICE MEMORANDUM

TO: *Harry T. (Peoria Plant)*
FROM: *Melvin C.*
SUBJECT: *Editing of Your Presentation*

1. I can well understand your dismay upon receiving a revised version of your recommendations on quality-control procedures. I am not going to debate whether your proposals have suffered or they have been distorted;

but I will admit that they were substantially rewritten by George Roberts.

2. Fundamentally, your original presentation is an excellent one which required some editing only (in a limited sense), and it was agreed that George would be given that task. As you know, George has recently completed quite a bit of research on the subject, and he has been drafting presentations for the systems department. I believe George's intentions were good and constructive, but I must admit that he perhaps went beyond the limits of the usual license that an editor has.

3. Let me get right to the point. I intend to have someone directly under my supervision make some of the changes which I believe will strengthen the presentation. This will be done immediately, so that you can submit it through channels as you had originally planned. You have already been delayed too long!

4. Harry, be assured that we do not want you to stop sending in proposals, nor do we want to have others do your writing for you. Your intention to speak and write freely are identical to the desires of the production methods committee. I can assure you that as long as I am active on the production methods committee, the systems function will not be permitted to sterilize any creative thinking from other sources. So, speak your mind and keep your ideas coming. We welcome them.

5. I believe it only fair to point out that George Roberts and the systems department have done an excellent job in producing high-quality recommendations and presentations. In the main, they are to be commended for an exceptionally fine job. Occasionally they may go astray, but perhaps all of us do at one time or another. Let's give them another chance.

6. You will be receiving a copy of the edited presentation from me in the near future.

7. I will be visiting your plant later this month and I look forward to chatting with you at that time.

(signed)

cc: G. Roberts
Production vice president
Director of the systems department
Peoria plant manager
General production manager
Ad hoc committee on quality control

On a first reading, George's reaction was prompt. "Who's he kidding? The little SOB is trying to take over systems." Although the cloak is transparent, and Melvin's intentions are obvious enough, there is still good reason to analyze the memo further in order to uncover the variety of tricks that were used.

To begin with, in Paragraphs 1 and 2, the memo twice ostensibly *admits* to things for which Melvin actually takes no responsibility. While pretending to admit errors, he's really accusing George. This sly twist is a common ploy that should never slip by unnoticed. It generally pays to scrutinize all purported admissions before going ahead with an analysis.

A second general observation concerned the memo's apparent praise for George's *intentions* (Paragraph 2) and *in the main . . . exceptionally fine job* (Paragraph 5). Actually, each of these statements is followed by a retraction. Then comes the effrontery of a plea that George be given *another chance!* When an appeal is not only specious, but heavy-handed as well, it screams *Foul!*

On a second, more careful reading of the memo, George ignored all the tricks and twists as he prepared an outline, paragraph by paragraph, putting on every statement a plausible, positively motivated construction, thus:

1. A softener for the addressee: *I understand.*
2. An alibi for the writer: *It wasn't my doing.*

3. Making amends to Harry: *We'll straighten things out promptly.*

4. Encouragement to Harry: *Go on doing what you've been doing.*

5. Pat on the back and slap on the wrist for George and the systems department: *They do a great job, but . . .*

6. Promise of prompt action, repeated: *. . . in the near future.*

7. Friendly close: *See you soon.*

Why does George bother to prepare an outline that strains against reason to credit the sender with the purest of intentions? Several good purposes are served by such an exercise: First, before George accuses anyone of acting out of dubious motives, he must protect his own flanks against a possible countercharge of unfairness or overreaction. So he works at being more than fair, frequently creating doubts and resolving them in favor of an adversary.

Second, George wants to comprehend his adversary's possible defenses. By deliberately construing statements as innocently as possible, George expects not only to turn up specific answers and denials the memo-writer will undoubtedly have ready, but, often, to perceive also the general outlines of the fortifications behind which he is planning to ensconce himself after his foray against George.

It is particularly important to exercise the greatest caution when a memo or its sender is slippery. Accordingly, George made no response: Melvin's potential defenses could hardly be called flimsy. He was merely trying to placate the injured Harry, restore harmony, and encourage good performance in the future. So George stored away, for his private use, the knowledge that Mel was not to be trusted. On his side, Melvin looked for a reaction from George, but none was forthcoming; and Melvin was not prone to suspect that George was aware of his duplicity.

Furthermore, George could see trouble brewing between

Harry and Mel, since the memo represented an unanticipated challenge to Harry's jealously guarded prerogatives. From George's standpoint, why not let the pot simmer?

Nevertheless, George did proceed with another reading of the memo, a reading designed to explore and evaluate the author's capabilities as an underhanded operative. George's next paragraph-by-paragraph outline goes out of its way to impute evil intent:

1. I am taking responsibility for the systems department, admitting errors on its behalf and acting as though I controlled its activities.

2. You're right and George is wrong.

3. I will see to it that things get done right, and promptly, too. That systems group can't really be trusted with a job; and they stall things besides.

4. Trust me, Harry; for I will be your friend and protector.

5. The systems department needs guidance from me. I respect them; I'm not out to get them; but they'd do well to follow me.

6. I'll show you—and Roberts—how to get things done properly.

7. Let's get together. Maybe we can keep the kettle boiling.

Manifestly, this outline is hostile, and George knew better than to make it the basis for a response. On the contrary, he held to his resolve and made no reply. George now uses the unflattering outline as a guide to Mel's mode of operations in other circumstances, just as criminologists find it useful to study the *modus operandi* of their subjects. Mel clearly needs watching.

The real message that comes out of a scrutiny of Mel's memorandum is that it doesn't work. The writer may think he is being subtle in fanning animosities while claiming friendship all around; but actually, the crudity of his game can only serve to alert the astute political operatives in his company to a danger in their midst. George has seen the warning signals of the Law of Aggrandizement, and so have others. Harry is both fearful and resentful of what he perceives as an attempt to usurp his prerogatives. If Mel never wrote another memorandum like this one, he would still be regarded with suspicion on every hand.

WHY A MEMO?

Think twice before sending a memorandum, if only because others will question its motives, perhaps reading into it ulterior objectives that were not intended. Additionally, the feedback will never be accurate and complete, so that the writer of a memo runs the risk of not finding out what impression he has created.

Yet another hazard lurks for the memo-writer. In every cautious reader's mind, questions arise: *Why a memo? Why did the writer choose to commit her thoughts to paper when she might have called or met with me instead?* In the case above, *Why did Mel choose to answer Harry by memo, with all those copies, instead of talking things over with George privately?* Those are good questions. After all, a conversation allows an exchange of information, immediate reactions, correction of misunderstandings, and modification of positions. The atmosphere can be relaxed and informal. Real blunders can be averted. Retreat is always possible. And written confirmation can follow. So why did the writer choose to communicate by memorandum instead?

There are legitimate reasons for writing, of course. To lay claim to an idea. To go on record. To explain a complex matter in depth. Nevertheless, when all the reasons are totted up, there is still cause for suspicion whenever anyone receives a memorandum. To put it bluntly, a memo is not simply a device for telling someone something. That can be done more easily by telephone. So why a memo?

Many memos are defensive: They are intended to get the writer off the hook. She issues a warning; and if things go wrong, she can wave her memo and say, "Don't look at me. I knew something was going to happen, and I said so." Or she may pass the buck, pointing later to her memo and saying, "I thought you were going to handle that matter. You didn't tell me you were sitting on my memo while the situation deteriorated." Perhaps she fires the first shot in an incipient controversy, hoping that her initial accusation will present her with an advantage. She may issue orders that throw over to the receiver of the memo the burden of taking measures to keep himself in the clear. *Even "the record" that is so often cited as the main reason for writing a memorandum is essentially defensive; few people knowingly prepare records that could be used against them.*

Defensive and doubtful as many reasons are for preparing memos, much that is written is encouraged by the Law of Rationalization and condoned by custom. But more disingenuous types of memorandum are conceived out of motives that are not notably benign. For example, Melvin's memorandum above was addressed to Harry, but the principal message—that the systems department should be put under Melvin's wing—was intended for some of the copied-in addressees. People who take the trouble to read memos carefully will discover that a considerable number of memos are not written for the ostensible (principal) addressees at all, but rather for someone else. It behooves every recipient of a memorandum to ask, *Is this message intended to put me on the spot with one of the other recipients?* Needless to say, whenever you find that blind copies have been sent to people not listed for distribution, you can be sure that there is some mischief afoot.

Look carefully for signs that the writer had another audience in mind: explanations of things you already know; a history of ill-starred events that you participated in; credit to you for achievements that another addressee might con-

sider dubious; or advice that you can't use, but another addressee would welcome or find admirable. If the writer has
you in mind as her sole reader, then she should be writing
things that will ingratiate her with you, influence you, persuade you to follow a certain course, or bring you into a
joint project. Failing all of these purposes, the chances are
good that the memo was never really intended for you in
the first place.

A truly devious use of memos is calculated to evoke a
response that can be distorted for reprehensible ends. Beware of baited hooks. George has concluded that the safest
way to handle most baited memos is to ignore the senders.
Formally responding to unfair attacks would only enmesh
him in a contest he can't win. If he were to go into the
memo-writing business, his legitimate activities would suffer,
and an observant management would eventually take note
of his derelictions. The obvious conclusion, an incongruity
with management's goals, could only be disastrous. Fortunately, informal contacts with other addressees is both more
effective and less risky in setting aright the distortions of a
tricky memorandum.

To sum up, it is a useful exercise to read each memorandum
carefully, objectively, and analytically. Ask what the memo
is intended to accomplish. Is it meant to produce action, to
gain support, to seek recognition, to resolve an issue, to explain a situation, to excuse the writer, or to express his
views? Then note how the writer goes about achieving his
goal. Finally, evaluate both the ends and the means. Are
they proper and honorable, or do they reflect incompetence
or culpability?

Notice also how people are treated by the writer: whether
there is an attempt to curry favor or to shift blame; whether
the writing is respectful or derogatory; whether anyone is
put into an awkward position, embarrassed, or subjected to
abuse. Examine the facts and implications, too. People of
integrity don't misrepresent, exaggerate, or disregard facts

in order to bolster their position. It is proper also to interpret every statement literally, as it is written. The writer who misuses words out of sheer negligence is presumed to be as culpable as the one who is guilty of deliberate misstatement.

Whenever people write, they select and marshal facts and opinions from a mass of data. As a natural course, many subjects must be skipped as the writer chooses some material for presentation and leaves out other, more or less relevant, matter. Furthermore, the selection process normally follows the Law of Self-Interest. Before completing your evaluation of each writer and his memo, ask what has been left unsaid. Given the background of the topic, what might have been included, but wasn't? Are the omissions significant; do they follow a pattern? If so, then what is the message that the omissions convey? These omissions may often speak louder, or send a more important message, than the memo itself. Every reader should develop a healthy curiosity about what has not been covered, as well as what has. Especially significant are those questions that have been previously raised and are disregarded now—neither answered nor acknowledged, but cavalierly dismissed or quietly neglected. Those issues tell a story of their own.

17

COMMITTEES, MEETINGS, AND CONVERSATIONS

OPERATING AT ITS BEST, a committee can be an effective instrument for overcoming certain obstacles. In a company, a committee whose members represent different departments can bring about a degree of coordination that would be difficult to achieve otherwise. In party politics, a committee representing diverse constituencies can hammer out compromises not readily attainable in any other way. The act of working together toward a common goal, combined with the opportunity for members to present their own views and listen to the opinions of others, can build a foundation capable of supporting a more elaborate structure of agreements.

Why do executives appoint committees? Ostensibly, to investigate a subject, report findings, and recommend a course of action (seldom to make decisions). By contrast, actual reasons may include tactics of buck-passing and delay, an earnest desire to share unwanted responsibility, or an effort to line up support. Thus the committee system is available for an assortment of uses and abuses by persons with disparate motives.

The committee system is inherently neither authoritarian nor democratic. It can work under either philosophy, and the turn it takes will be determined by the outlook and methods of the people involved. A committee is the focal point of three sets of political interests: the appointing authority, the chairperson, and the individual members. Interactions are influenced by the character of the committee: *standing* or *ad hoc*. Membership associations operate through a permanent structure of standing committees, which predominate. Ad hoc committees may be appointed to pursue specific matters—and they may be very important—but it is the standing committees, created under the by-laws, that provide associations with continuity of operations. By contrast, a typical business corporation has few standing committees; most of its committees are ad hoc. In all types of organizations, the appointing authority for standing committees is generally an officer, board, or committee acting under a charter, often in accordance with precedent or protocol; whereas ad hoc committees are created by individuals or groups with considerable latitude.

THE APPOINTING AUTHORITY

The first to put his imprint on an ad hoc committee is the appointing authority. His purpose may be to have the committee confirm his own convictions. After naming reliable people, he feels secure in the committee's predisposition to put down dissent. Then why does he bother to appoint a committee at all? For several reasons. If his company espouses democracy, a committee maintains appearances. Also, committee members can go forth with messages like missionaries among their less-enlightened fellows.

Then there is the executive who appoints committees in order to relieve himself of the arduous tasks of weighing data, establishing criteria, and considering alternative courses. This abdication of authority, in favor of the virtual anonymity of committee compromises, is not to everyone's taste; but it fills a need for some. The committee system cloaks their indecisiveness and enables them to dodge responsibility.

While the dodgers are even more comfortable as members of committees than as appointing authorities or chairpersons, not every committee is a refuge for the timid. Aggressive leadership sometimes asserts itself and carries a committee into an activist posture. Also, while members abandon individual responsibility, a committee as a whole may acquire a standing of its own, permitting the group to act with a boldness the individual members lack. Thus it is that a committee, under prodding, sometimes bands together to confound those who had counted on its docility.

To head off an unwelcome turn of events, the appointing authority may issue directives to the chairperson and hold him responsible for quelling ferment. However, if a committee should take its ostensible duties seriously, managing somehow to discharge its announced functions objectively, then it behooves the appointing executive to take heed, under the Law of Constraints. When responsible people knowingly act contrary to the wishes of a power source, they are sending a particularly strong message.

Therein lies the latent threat of a committee: Using its prestige and manpower, the committee can promote an idea that has been anathema to the company and to the appointing authority. Such things do happen. Hence the reluctance of authoritarians to appoint committees on matters of consequence. A less rigid appointing authority may seek to exercise personal control (an abuse of the chairperson), or he may hold the chairperson responsible for the committee's conformity to the Establishment's design (another form of abuse).

THE CHAIRPERSON

If the chairperson is not so abused but finds himself neglected and uninformed, then he must evaluate the situation, drawing from the appointing authority as much information as possible. Similarly, if the chairperson chooses to withhold information from his allies on the committee, then they are compelled to watch for indications of his intent. A committee without direction cannot be criticized for going off in peculiar directions. The onus belongs to those who neglected to pass the message along in the right places, for their fear of exercising power has burdened the committee unnecessarily.

The chairperson in pursuit of legitimate objectives can make the committee system work for him. He should have the right to select other members of his committee, or at least to influence their selection. Undoubtedly, he will favor certain kinds of people. A chairperson should refrain from appointing members whose previous contributions have been negligible or negative. Assuming that he truly wants to resolve controversial issues by a process that includes discussion and negotiation, then his committee should comprise people of diverse opinions, including potential critics of possible decisions, representatives of major constituencies that will be affected by the committee's decisions, and disinterested, informed persons. If such a group does reach an agreement, it can be made to stick. That's important.

When the members of a committee have accepted appointment, the chairperson solicits their suggestions and advice, which he then disseminates to all members for comment. An agenda should be sent to committee members in advance of each meeting, along with a draft of the minutes of the previous meeting. Everything should be done to give each member a feeling that he is being informed of developments, that all are participating in the decision process. The risk to the chairperson is that members with a predilection for criticism will flourish.

That risk is real, for committees are peculiarly vulnerable to criticism from within. Left uncontrolled, a single critic can make himself a noisome impediment. The chairperson should be able to call on supporters to counteract detrimental activities. General, vague criticism should be challenged with requests for clarification. The chair's allies should volley the ball back to the complainer's court, where it belongs.

Negative criticism requires insistence on constructive suggestions. For, no matter how well-meaning critics may be, they have not done justice to themselves until they have wrestled with their problems, analyzing exactly where the difficulties lie and working out possible solutions. That discipline will be good medicine for dissenters. The chairperson's job is to prescribe the administration of ample dosage. Specific criticism and suggestions have to be categorized according to their validity. For the sake of harmony, innocuous suggestions should be allocated some space—but not much.

Harmful notions present a different sort of problem. Sometimes critics can be persuaded to relinquish them. At other times, meaningless substitutes may succeed in preventing disruption.

In all committee work, it is important to get as many points as possible resolved by private negotiation beforehand, so that committee meetings tend to ratify agreements instead of degenerating into controversy, bitterness, and humiliating defeat for either side. It is easier to work out compromises before positions are announced publicly. The larger the committee, the greater the chairperson's need to know how members are thinking. It is risky to allow a persuasive speaker to turn her charismatic powers loose, unopposed, on a group that might succumb to deceptive arguments.

In party politics, experienced professionals are seldom willing to take their chances on the outcome of a vote they have not attempted to influence beforehand. They know—or believe they know—the sentiment of nearly all the delegates, and they are ready to predict privately the outcome of a vote. Rather than suffer a damaging defeat, they'll usually withdraw. When they decide to move forward, they are seldom wrong. Surely, if a floor leader needs to count in advance of a meeting, a chairperson should be no less well informed.

Despite efforts to reach agreements, a chairperson may have to deal with recalcitrant committee members. With adequate preparation, he can not only carry it off but also boost his own stock. Lone obstructionists tend to arouse resentment toward themselves and consolidate the rest of the committee behind the chairperson. With such an advantage, the chair can afford to be forbearing and gracious toward disrupters. The chairperson's defensive plays should always be carried out away from meetings. At meetings, he can only be patient and pleasant, concentrating always on augmenting the influence he has on the rest of the committee.

However, even while being pleasant, a chairperson can avail himself of methods for keeping committee members in line. Time-allocations, derived by dividing the estimated length of the meeting first by the number of subjects on the agenda, and then by the number of members present, should be used. No member can be held rigidly to such an allocation, but the concept of a time-allocation for each member to speak on a single subject can help in limiting discussion reasonably.

It is the chairperson's responsibility to control talkative fools by noting when they stray from issues or repeat themselves. For the most part, chairpersons learn how to stop rambling rather quickly in business, government, and the professions. The problem of the garrulous egotist is more likely to plague the community organization whose chairperson lacks a requisite toughness.

It is appropriate for the chair to assume that any member

who offers a suggestion involving work intends to volunteer his own services. In general, his assignment to the suggested project should be confirmed with promptness and gratitude, for he has earned the right to be so assigned. An extension of this device calls for assigning a critic to a subcommittee he has attacked, ostensibly as an opportunity for him to exert a beneficial influence, but actually to lead him into responsible conduct or, as some would have it, to shut him up.

To summarize: Ideally, agreements should be reached before each meeting. Then, at the meeting, each side speaks for the record. Preferably, the speakers are designated in advance. With all these arrangements settled, there should be no difficulty in finishing the meeting's business within the allotted time. Normal courtesies may be extended to recalcitrants with the hope that they will actively participate in the group's work. With properly laid plans, meetings can generally be conducted in an orderly manner, despite occasional disruptive tactics.

THE COMMITTEE MEMBER

Getting appointed to the right committees is an important part of politicking, and sometimes a rather difficult one. It may be necessary to become known to someone with authority to make committee appointments, or to someone who is in a position to recommend appointments. The next step is to make one's interest in committee work known, and if necessary, to have others speak in one's behalf. Appointment to a committee should be considered not as an honor, but rather as an opportunity to broaden contacts and earn the respect of the other members. Cooperation with a committee and its chairperson should bring new appointments. Hence, the most important goal of a committee member is to project a good image among her colleagues. On a company committee, she has a chance to make friends of people in other departments, most likely people at her own level. (The rigidity of the caste system varies from one company to another.) Meeting with them for lunch, discussing committee affairs with them, is good politicking.

Susan Williams takes every precaution to present herself as a knowledgeable, reasonable person who gets along well with others. Avoiding identification with persistent dissenters, refusing to be gulled into untenable positions, and chary of offering opinions she's not prepared to support with facts, Susan keeps her guard up at committee meetings.

From the standpoint of furthering the committee's work, a member's most important contact is usually with the chair, and not solely because of the Law of Influence. The chairperson carries the chief responsibility and receives the lion's share of the recognition for results, but chairpersons need help. They must prepare agendas, recognize speakers, direct and summarize discussions, and appoint subcommittees. Assisting chairpersons and acting agreeably are good strategies for committee members. For a specific appointment, talk to the chairperson. To put an item on the next agenda, suggest it to the chair. Whatever your position or your intentions, it's a good idea to keep the chair informed, so that he won't be confronted with surprises at meetings. Exchange ideas with him, and he may be able to help round up support. Grateful chairpersons can get you assignments to other, perhaps more desirable, committees.

Whenever Susan is the lone woman among men, her long conditioning prompts her to record the minutes of the meeting. In what is almost a reflex action by the chairperson, she is promptly appointed secretary. The designation as secretary gives Susan a certain prominence, which is enhanced by her reading the minutes at the next meeting and signing them for the record. Additionally, she has a chance to demonstrate her grasp of essentials and her skill in articulating them. She is also brought closer to the chairperson. Although Susan feels a justifiable resentment at the equation *woman equals secretary,* she ought not to let that resentment blind her to reality: Relinquishing a worthwhile prize would be a futile gesture. It's better to let the men on the committee fight to wrest that prize away—when they come to recognize its value.

Unfortunately, a chairperson who is wrong for the job can frustrate your efforts. Incompetents can surface anywhere. In particular, pompous types seem to be drawn to the opportunities afforded a chairperson. Arrogantly setting themselves up as authorities on all matters, they repeatedly inject their own views during committee discussions. Characteristically, they disdain facts and prefer to impose their opinions, instead.

What can a committee member do when the chairperson overdominates discussions and otherwise throws his weight around? Watch the attitudes of other members, and listen carefully for potential allies. Sound out those people on important issues before the next meeting. Organize the opposition. If you have the votes, you can beat any chairperson. If you don't have the votes, you will have to live under a tyrannical rule until the chair's tactics, or the unpopularity of a specific proposal, drive a majority over to your side. It's that simple. But don't make the mistake of forcing an open confrontation at a meeting when your side can't win. Pitting your ego against the chairperson's is useless.

TACTICS AT MEETINGS

Although it is a poor tactic for an individual to monopolize a discussion or hold the floor for extended periods, it can still be useful to one's image as a leader to speak longer than others do. Nevertheless, wasting people's time with trivia will earn a reputation as a bore. The right procedure is to elaborate each comment into a statement of appropriate length, with introduction, announcement of a point, suitable development, restatement, and close. Each separate thought is entitled to the equivalent of a paragraph of writing, plus the repetition that the spoken word permits.

As in everything else, Arthur Gordon watches for feedback. Since his audience frequently looks to him for opinions, he assumes that his method for presenting material is succeeding; but if people acted impatient every time he began to talk, the verdict would be clear. He often gets a mixed reaction: Opponents are not eager to welcome statements coming from the other side, and that doesn't worry him. He speaks for his friends and allies, while addressing his remarks to the uncommitted group, hoping to win over some of them. It is a delusion to think that a confirmed opponent will be swayed by the logic of one's argument, the magic of one's voice, or the cogency of one's presentation. Opponents have their own motives for holding to their beliefs, and it's unrealistic to expect that they will give others a fair hearing. Arthur has long ago given up attempts at converting opponents.

A favorite tactic for retaining control is for the controlling side to take more time than it allows the opposition. More speakers are presented, and each takes all the time allotted to him. A crude controlling group may be found dominating the early discussion and then imposing time limits on later speakers. However, if the ruse is too obvious, it may fail by offending the sense of fairness of an uncommitted group. Speaking time is important, but it isn't the sole determining factor in decision-making. Other considerations are more compelling in the end.

Many meetings are insufferable. While attempting to broaden one's contacts and build a favorable image, it is often necessary to sit through tedious sessions. Accordingly, when the monotonous drone of one member, the asinine objections of another, the quibbles of a third, and the bombast of a fourth mount to an unbearable pitch, just relax. Don't take it all so seriously. Keep your perspective and sense of humor. Remember that the primary purpose in attending meetings is political—and the attainment of your goals is not hampered by others' making fools of themselves.

For a person who is privy to the political maneuvers of one side or another, meetings seldom become dull. Boredom indicates a failure to do one's homework. Before the next meeting, it will be necessary to find out where the action is behind the scenes. Meanwhile, when a meeting becomes unbearable, the immediate problem calls for turning to personal amusements. Some people sketch or doodle; some carry around crossword puzzles, cryptograms, word games, or mathematical exercises. Such diverse activities as knitting and vocabulary-building help others while away the time profitably. At large meetings, people read or work out magic squares.

A more constructive game for avoiding boredom—while maintaining appearances—is to test your understanding of people and speculate as to their alliances. Follow up by taking note of switches and by interpreting each change in position. Guess who belongs to each group by watching patterns of expressed support and patterns of voting. During discussions, observe the byplay; catch the side remarks, the small conferences, the exchanges of winks and nods. Look for other nonverbal indications of agreement, disagreement, indifference, or annoyance. A study of byplay and individual reactions combines entertainment with usefulness. It's an eye-opener, in more ways than one.

LISTENING AND OBSERVING

Considering the critical importance of information in politicking—its importance can scarcely be overrated—and the lengths to which companies and individuals go to acquire data, it would be an unconscionable waste to let information in one's possession slip away.

At first, Susan Williams found it difficult to cull the essentials of discussions from the chaff, and her notes were voluminous. With practice, she learned to listen for topic sentences and summaries—the essential ingredients of economical note-taking.

Susan once resented dull lecturers, but now she remains alert by staying ahead of such speakers, anticipating the direction of their remarks. When a speaker surprises Susan with something she had not expected, she jots down a note or two. Later, when the speaker gets back on a familiar path, Susan turns once more to anticipating the line of reasoning and waiting for the next unexpected departure. After all, the departures are what she can learn from, and what she wants to retain.

Whether listening to a formal address or engaging in a conversational exchange, Susan analyzes each speaker's motives, listening for clues to determine what the speaker is trying to accomplish. She also judges the speaker's comprehension of his subject, his flexibility and willingness to adjust his positions, the adequacy of his preparation, and his openness.

Paying attention and raising the right questions are not the whole story, however. Having captured information, Susan must store it. Immediately after a meeting of any sort (including serious conversations), she prepares a record for her files, which now contain invaluable material for defensive purposes and politicking in general. There's nothing like a record committed to writing at once; reliance on memory is not nearly as good, as recollections tend to grow fuzzy. Anyone who is unconvinced on this score should try an experiment: First, record the business transacted at a meeting, and set these notes aside for several months. Then try once more to record what had transpired at the same meeting. Finally, compare the two records and discover for yourself how much valuable information had slipped from your memory.

Records of meetings and conversations lend continuity to

communications. Whenever Susan has occasion to meet with the same individuals again, she briefs herself on the content of previous proceedings and related conversations, including personal notes. In addition, whenever fresh information casts new light on a past exchange, or on the motives of a participant, her notes permit a reevaluation and a fresh interpretation of hidden messages. However, since preparation of detailed notes can be onerous, time pressures may cause occasional lapses even among the most disciplined of people. So Susan keeps a diary on her desk for jotting down brief comments or outlines after all discussions. Better to have a few sketchy notes than nothing at all; and a diary's chronological arrangement of entries is advantageous, too. When the telephone rings, Susan has a pad handy for recording the caller's name and affiliation, important references, key words, and essential comments. At the end of a significant telephone conversation, she prepares a more detailed record for her diary or file, just as with any other conversation.

Along with many other women, Susan encounters men who won't listen to her. There isn't much she can do about it. However, the problem is not really hers—or won't be for long. Since women will be increasingly influential in administrative circles, holding positions of power in greater numbers, any man who tunes women out is headed for trouble. Those men who cannot bring themselves to seek business advice from women had better change their ways. Their period of grace is running out.

It has become fashionable to pay particular attention to *nonverbal clues* as to a speaker's motives, attitudes, and personality. Telltale signs supposedly provide insights not otherwise available: what this person does with his hands while he talks or listens, the way that person cocks her head, or the fact that she crosses her legs. To be sure, gestures and attitudes have always been scrutinized for the secrets they might betray. Impatience is easily recognized, and so is preoccupation with other matters. Shifting, turning away, and becoming distracted are bad omens. As tension builds, listen for throat-clearing and changes in the pitch of voices; and watch those hands as they move about, play with objects, and clench into tight fists. Common sense is the best guide to many valuable observations.

However, caution should be exercised before accepting correlations derived from insufficient observation of subjects. Assuredly, specific gestures may appear to be related to attitudes, but supporting evidence is meager.

Furthermore, the validity of conclusions may easily be upset by design. Be wary of people who apply themselves to learning the "right" gestures as a means for manipulating those "sophisticates" who obligingly stake everything on knowledge of the latest and most esoteric fads. Gullibility is never so dangerous as when compounded by a fatuous presumption of sophistication.

18

SPIDER ON A
FLYWHEEL

ORGANIZATIONS ARE indispensable and essentially neutral, so far as people are concerned. Politicking is conducted between people; the company, as such, is not involved in internal politicking. It merely provides a structure and setting within which people operate. Moreover, no organization of any size can long remain truly monolithic, for its people are moved by forces pulling in divergent directions. Individual plans are laid, roles are assayed, designs are executed, and plots and subplots thicken and unfold as in a grand, continuous play in a theater with many stages. Meanwhile, the company's purposes are served or disserved in varying degree by these individual activities.

It is not far-fetched to ascribe a *personality* of sorts to a company. As Susan looked into companies of all sizes, she readily discerned differences in attitude, manner, and outlook. On the surface, there might be coldness or warmth, optimism or pessimism, energy or lethargy, orderliness or confusion, thoughtfulness or foolishness, courtesy or rudeness, encouragement or discouragement. Underneath, there were less obvious, but more important, differences in integrity, concern, adaptability, and momentum.

FLYWHEEL AND GYROSCOPE

Over short periods of normal operation, a typical company's personality remains stable. The management may exhibit several facets, only one of which can dominate; and it may successfully hide duplicitous activities from naïve newcomers. Nevertheless, the traits that add up to a personality resist abrupt change. On the contrary, in this and many another matter, *companies have built-in flywheels of conservatism that regulate the rate of change, whether induced by internal or external forces.* The larger the company, the larger the flywheel, and the greater the inertial tendency.

Whether the flywheel effect will be comforting or frustrating to an individual depends on his point of view in a given situation. If an impending change is perceived as a threat to one's interests, then the flywheel takes on the appearance of a beneficent, protective mechanism. But when your most fervently cherished hopes are delayed, then the flywheel looms as a fiendish device that willfully impedes progress and exasperates people. Actually, the flywheel itself is neither good nor evil.

As bicycle-riders know, a wheel which is spinning—such as a flywheel in motion—exhibits a gyroscopic effect. Thus, when a bicycle rider leans to either side, the bicycle in motion resists tumbling to the ground: It changes direction instead. More generally, when a wheel is spinning, any pressure exerted to induce a change in the axle's direction is converted into a force which moves the axle in a different plane. So it is with companies. *Attempts to change a company's course in one direction frequently end up in an unanticipated shift with a different intent.* Most often, this gyroscopic effect is a manifestation of the Laws of Aggrandizement, Group Survival, and Power. Individuals make suggestions to benefit themselves, others introduce modifications to suit their interests, and at the end of a negotiating process, a proposal emerges that is represented as enhancing the survival prospects of the company as a whole, or of dominant interests within it. The original intent is generally lost in the process.

In formulating plans for oneself or for the company, there are few images more useful than the flywheel, with its gyroscopic concomitant. The size of the flywheel—and hence its momentum and inertia—depends on the size of the company. A flywheel's resistance to change is inexorable, for it has no capacity to act in any other way than its nature dictates. If an individual is out of phase with his company, it is the individual who will be pressured to adapt.

The Law of Constraints limits the effectiveness of individuals in a great many matters, and the inertial tendency of the flywheel reinforces the resistance to fundamental change in a company's personality most of all. In companies of all sizes, *the flywheel effect is strongest when the corporate personality is the subject of a proposed change.*

People owe it to themselves, before joining any kind of organization, to investigate its personality. It is too much to expect that anyone, at any level, will be able to reform an organization rapidly by converting large numbers of its people to a new philosophy. Regardless of the reformers' idealism or ruthlessness, it is also unrealistic to expect that reforms can be instituted without the consent of large numbers of people.

For the most part, an individual spends his organizational life like a spider on a flywheel. Once he gets used to the steady motion, he goes about his business among the spokes, feeling little of either the flywheel effect or the gyroscope effect. These forces make themselves felt only on those occasions when you attempt a change in the company's destinies. Rightly or wrongly, most efforts are routinely directed at continuity of operations, not change. The spider on a flywheel is the standard of behavior for those who have accepted the organizational pattern. Since contrary behavior is sure to be condemned, it is unsafe for an individualist to flout the comfortable norms, especially when, in the eyes of nearly everyone else, they derive from the Law of Group Survival or the Law of Power.

GOAL-CONGRUENCE

Companies display personality differences whose origins are obscure. In observing how people interact within an organizational setting, it becomes apparent that executives are held up as behavioral models—sometimes catastrophically. Honorable dealings at the top, it is reasoned, are likely to foster a sense of honor throughout. In the more usual situation, managerial duplicity engenders deceit among employees in their dealings, not only with management but also among themselves and with outsiders. Much of a company's distinctive personality reflects management's manner of carrying out its responsibilities, as the attitudes of people in the company reflect their perceptions of management: its actions, attitudes, and directions.

Management's basic responsibility is to formulate and pursue major objectives by mobilizing, deploying, and utilizing company resources. For the purposes of this discussion, it will suffice to recall the usual mnemonic categories of management theory—*the four M's*—for describing these resources: manpower, machinery, materials, and money. Of these four factors, our present interest is primarily in manpower: the people who make the machines run (or stand idle); who purchase, convert, sell (or waste) materials; who raise, use (or squander) money. All the apparatus and the paraphernalia of management—organization charts, operating manuals, communication networks, and status symbols—are directed toward bringing people together to promote the goals of the enterprise. To the extent that a method fails in that undertaking, it is either useless or detrimental. All of management's directives must serve to coordinate activities in pursuit of common goals, or they too are unnecessary. The effectiveness of the leadership must be judged in terms of its achieving congruence between parochial goals and overall objectives. For it is management's obligation to reconcile individual aspirations to the good of the corporate entity.

It is an individual's responsibility—and not the company's —to avoid situations involving irreconcilable conflict between personal convictions and company objectives, operations, or products. In illustrations that are clear-cut, a person who condemns cigarette-smoking should not work for a tobacco company, and a person who opposes the drinking of hard liquor should not take a job with a distillery. But most questions are not so easily resolved. After working for a toy-maker for many years, a person may one day find that her employer has been bought out by a cigarette-manufacturer. If she is deeply disturbed by the prospect of being associated with a new employer that promotes smoking, her ethical problem is very real. What position should a person take on the question of working for a bank that services a notorious polluter? The ramifications of these problems are staggering.

To satisfy one's conscience, it is perhaps sufficient, before joining a company, to ascertain that it acts in ways that are apparently honorable. To illustrate, if you are concerned about the social consequences of a prospective employer's operations, then find out where it stands on environmental protection, employment practices, community relations, and so on. And don't overlook the good that it does by offering useful products and services.

FRUSTRATION

It is easy to see how personal aspirations can be frustrated by corporate goal congruence, flywheel inertia, and gyroscopic perverseness. To these facts of corporate life must be added those sources of frustration that originate with systemic defects, for frustration feeds on overlapping responsibilities, failure to communicate, narrow specializing, and fragmented work. People at lower levels obviously have a twin problem of boredom and frustration; but at higher levels also, pedestrian chores, routine, and helplessness to change things are resented—despite efforts by systems experts to invest work with meaning.

When accumulated frustration brings you near the boiling point, and rage threatens to overcome your good judgment, remember that you are not alone. Frustration is the main characteristic of individuals in business. Nevertheless, many of the specific suggestions in this book can help to forestall or moderate your personal frustration. Investigating a company's personality and leadership style before joining is a most important preventive measure. Maintaining good relations with—belonging to—a group, and a grapevine, rank high. Gaining satisfaction through successful innovation can help those who are willing to take risks.

Then there is an attitude that can help. Look upon your relations with your boss and company as a continual process of negotiation. Regarding the company as your adversary, establish your minimum demands and negotiate constantly for more. When you lose a point, as you will, try another tack. If you can be temporarily satisfied with the minimum you have established, if you can be patient in your attempts to secure greater gains, and if you are able to shrug off temporary defeat as you plan your next moves—then frustration will be less severe for you. On the other hand, if your minimum demands of the company are not met, then separate yourself from your surroundings emotionally, divest yourself of all feelings of loyalty, know that you are only marking time—and look for another job.

Short of leaving, you can try to invest your work, and your department's work, with meaning—without practicing a great deal of self-deception. Now put everything in perspective, with home, family, friends, hobbies, and community affairs offset against your job and reducing its relative importance in your life. Pick your outside interests and activities carefully so that they satisfy your unfulfilled needs, and you can be assured that you have done your best to cope with the human condition.

INDIVIDUAL PATTERNS

It becomes apparent that, sooner or later, a thinking individual will not be content to remain a spider on a flywheel. He must consider his relations with his company and his part in formulating, accepting, or disagreeing with ends and means. On the one hand, the individual contributes to the company's personality by the Law of Influence. On the other hand, the scope of his actions is officially prescribed by the company and unofficially circumscribed by the Law of Constraints.

There are analogies, of course. An individual must relate in some way to groups and organizations in many spheres. He must, for example, find his place in society. Will he conform or rebel? Will he assume an active or a passive role? Will he be a joiner or a loner? Will he lead or be led? Will he seek power or merely acceptance? Will his actions be grounded in altruism or selfishness? Will he adhere to an underlying conservative outlook or a liberal one?

Perhaps no one makes these decisions consciously, except on rare occasions. For the most part, people make immediate decisions without speculating on philosophical issues. Nevertheless, as specific options are daily accepted or rejected and decisions aggregate, patterns do emerge. Moreover, an individual's pattern shows a certain consistency, whether expressed at a PTA meeting in a discussion of racial integration, in a political organization as a volunteer worker for a candidate, or in a professional committee pondering a course of action for the year ahead.

An individual's selection of voluntary associations and activities is part of his pattern, provided that he is free to join or not to join. However, community pressures and the persuasion of friends are not easily shut out; in addition to such subtle influences are the distortions caused by inertia and informational gaps or lags. Furthermore, many organizations impinge on one's way of life to greater or lesser degree, whether one chooses to participate in their deliberations or not. Notably, political parties, through the government apparatus, affect people's lives whether they join, remain independently aloof, or become disdainfully apathetic. Those who neglect to vote on Election Day are still required to pay taxes, obey the laws that are passed, and live in the social climate those laws produce. Similarly, those who limit their participation in the electoral process, by abstaining from the party primaries, are no less subject to the full impact of governmental actions. Additionally, lobbyists and voluntary groups influence the options and trade-offs that daily affect everyone. For instance, environmental groups affect decisions concerning clean air *v.* energy, clear water *v.* "free" industrial waste-disposal, and wildlife preservation *v.* alternative land-use. While the conscientious citizen in a democracy is free to make certain choices, no one can escape the consequences of a decision to abstain from active participation.

Nor can a true romantic expect a cordial welcome in business. That's too bad, really, because romanticism helps to make the human condition tolerable for many good people; while a harsh materialism, pervasively institutionalized, is the curse of our society. Outside of eleemosynary and educational organizations, and a few islands in government, leadership positions for romantics are scarce. In business, they are thwarted by people with less imagination but more acceptance of their surroundings and of the Law of Aggrandizement.

For an individual in our society, the answer to helplessness is not to remove oneself from the scene, but rather to select suitable avenues for self-expression—organizations with compatible personalities—to make one's contribution, and to be patient. The effectiveness of that contribution can be enhanced by politicking in accordance with the Laws of Organizations.

DEMOCRACY IN BUSINESS

Comparisons between the political and the economic spheres reveal both similarities and dissimilarities. A salaried employee is free to change jobs. There are no legal restrictions on the scope of his search, the negotiations he enters into, or his freedom to leave his previous employment. And yet, qualified women and members of minority groups find that they are discriminated against in a great many areas of employment, sometimes openly and on frivolous grounds, but most often covertly. Discriminatory pay differentials and virtual exclusion from high-level positions are surely the most galling of all unfair employment practices, to use the legal terminology.

Few people are free to change jobs at will. Only by establishing a reputation for possessing unique talents that are in substantial demand, is it possible to extend one's mobility. Otherwise, the restraints imposed, in a free-enterprise system, by the subtle operation of the Invisible Hand of the marketplace, are real and cogent. Moreover, the condition of the job market determines the relative difficulty of a job search. Let the economy falter, and opportunities for changing jobs are curtailed. Indeed, the number of jobs advertised is a useful measure of economic activity.

Despite similarities, direct comparisons between business and government are perilous, and arguments that transfer concepts from either segment to the other must be regarded with suspicion. In particular, political democracy has little relevance to business management. The protection of individual freedom is sufficient justification for preferring democracy in government; but unless industry and government are virtually one, basic freedoms are not at stake in managing most businesses. In other words, unless government controls business or vice versa, political theory is largely irrelevant to business management.

Certain exceptions should be noted. First, where dissemination of news is the purpose of a business enterprise, perhaps even where communications are involved in a broader sense, a cogent argument can be made for democracy in management. Second, it can be argued that the future of political freedom would be more secure if giant industrial units were democratically managed. Third, a carryover of habits and thought processes might strengthen the foundations of democratic government in an intangible way if individual experience with nongovernmental organizations tended to reinforce democratic ideals on all sides. However, all these discussions are outside the scope of this book.

All things considered, it is realistic to cede to the management of a company the right to choose the kind of structure and the style of leadership that it judges to be most effective in holding its own against competition. In the exercise of these broad prerogatives, top management will have difficulty enough in controlling operations and accomplishing its objectives. To further enjoin top management would serve no useful purpose.

SELF-ASSERTION

How much should a company pay its employees? Beginning with the president, after taking into account company size, industry statistics, and the nature and magnitude of problems; and after evaluating education, experience, and ability required to do the job, the company still does not have an absolute measure. Likewise, the work of others in the organization down to the lowest levels—the base of the pyramid—cannot be evaluated by truly objective standards (although a subsistence level was once accepted as axiomatic by economists). But compensation is not wholly arbitrary, either; every economy has its own way of setting salaries, wages, and fringe benefits. In a free-enterprise system, the Invisible Hand of the labor market, influenced by labor unions and other organizations, as well as wage-and-hour laws, is presumed to govern the agreements by which people are paid for their services. In a slave economy, slave markets determine the prices paid for future services. Under dictatorships, government fiat controls. But always there is an understanding that the compensation for a specific job lies within a certain range, which may be either broad or narrow. And always the determination has been reached under conditions in which political pressures were influential or bargaining established the advantage that one side or group held over another. Consequently, every economic system works to the advantage of some groups and the disadvantage of others.

Perhaps the most mystifying of injustices are the strictures that males have imposed on females. There can be no doubt that women have all the requisites for overturning the system that has operated against them. They have the intelligence, the leadership, and the self-reliance to mount a massive assault on the economic, legal, and religious barriers that still confront them.

An objective assessment of modern society would have to conclude that the tide is running strong for fair treatment of those who have suffered inequities. In Western societies at least, social justice may yet become the guiding star for political and economic decisions. However, this book is directed to the concerns of individuals rather than groups. Our focus has been less on the prospects for social evolution than on the question, *How are you as an individual to survive and prosper?* To your knowledge of how organizations work, the following rules are added:

First, accept no limitations on yourself. Don't let anyone tell you that you're doing all right *for a woman* or *considering your background*. People of your own sex, race, or origin may be the worst offenders, outwardly at any rate.

Second, be a doer. Make things happen, instead of waiting to see what's in store for you next. You are a person, not a machine; a human being, not a cow. You have a heroic potential. Set reasonable goals and go after them, step by step. Get help if you can; go it alone if you have to. Accept reverses gracefully, without vindictiveness; retire to the sidelines occasionally to reassess your strategy; but get back in the game with fresh plans. Remember always that winning is best, losing a good fight is second best, and only losing by default bears the stigma of disgrace.

EPILOGUE

LIKE SNOW UPON
THE DESERT

FOR THE INDIVIDUAL to make the most of opportunities within an organization, he must understand how that organization works and how people operate within its structure. Management theory and practice are relevant to that understanding. However, several factors make management theory fluid and management practice erratic. First, the modern study of management is new in many respects, and dependent upon other disciplines that are themselves new, like industrial and social psychology. Naturally, in the early stages of theoretical development, change is often rapid, and experts frequently disagree.

Second, management theory is supported by very little study that can qualify as scientific research. In the main, practitioners' and consultants' insights are derived from uncontrolled observation or subjective experience. Simultaneously, much misinformation is disseminated, and many false starts lead nowhere as fads come and go.

Third, practicing managers, by and large, are neither sufficiently versed in nor committed to such precepts as have been reliably formulated. Consequently, progress in management methods is slower than need be, while misunderstandings and malpractice abound, often abetted by the herd instinct.

Despite the primitive state of *scientific management* and the slow pace of progress, improvements have come, and great strides will undoubtedly follow. Nevertheless, for present use the individual needs a guide that will help him or her examine with insight the consequences of particular policies and practices. This book has sought to provide such guidance.

With a proper guide, the individual can enter political games equipped for survival. Since the stakes are high, the game must be taken seriously. Fortunately, a serious attitude contributes to a player's enjoyment. And yet, a proper perspective must be maintained by the participants. They must be careful not to take *themselves* too seriously.

The risk of losing lends excitement to the game. Corruption and collusion are hard to beat. Rigged situations cannot always be sensed in time to avoid them. Opponents may be able to outflank, outmaneuver, and outstrip a player legitimately. Chance factors may upset the most detailed calculations. In the end, the best that an astute, alert, experienced player can do is to improve his odds and hope for the best.

Accordingly, it is well at the outset to temper one's ambitions with the reflection that an individual is not likely to build a lasting monument, no matter how skillfully he plays the game. In the words of Omar:

> The Worldly Hope men set their Hearts upon
> Turns Ashes—or it prospers, and anon,
>   Like Snow upon the Desert's dusty Face,
> Lighting a little hour or two—was gone.

ALLEN WEISS

A misfit all his life, Allen Weiss grew up in New York City (the Bronx) with a longing for the great outdoors. He majored in mathematics when it was considered an unpractical study, continued in accounting, became a CPA and, eventually, a management consultant among auditors. Moving upward in companies small, medium, and large to the financial officer level, he endured the puffery of little people and the pettiness of big ones. By a strange quirk, he enjoyed both military and civil service, working among engineers, psychologists, and statisticians. Adding close-up observations of inside party politics to his checkered career, Allen Weiss discovered the Natural Laws of Organizations and all that follows from them. He has also ghostwritten several books and articles, and edited professional journals.

Having lived in several parts of the country, he and his wife now make their home in suburban New Jersey.